The Industrial Revolution 1750–1850

The Industrial Revolution (1958) examines the various interpretations of early industrialization in Britain. It assesses and synthesizes the many writings on the industrial revolution to produce an insightful essay that spans the theories and thinking on the subject.

The Industrial Revolution
1750–1850

An Introductory Essay

H.L. Beales

Routledge
Taylor & Francis Group

First published in 1928
by Longmans, Green & Co. Ltd.
Second edition published in 1958
by Frank Cass & Co. Ltd.

This edition first published in 2025 by Routledge
4 Park Square, Milton Park, Abingdon, Oxon, OX14 4RN

and by Routledge
605 Third Avenue, New York, NY 10017

Routledge is an imprint of the Taylor & Francis Group, an informa business

Publisher's Note
The publisher has gone to great lengths to ensure the quality of this reprint but points out that some imperfections in the original copies may be apparent.

Disclaimer
The publisher has made every effort to trace copyright holders and welcomes correspondence from those they have been unable to contact.

A Library of Congress record exists under LCCN 28031193

ISBN: 978-1-032-90622-5 (hbk)
ISBN: 978-1-003-55894-1 (ebk)
ISBN: 978-1-032-90625-6 (pbk)

Book DOI 10.4324/9781003558941

THE INDUSTRIAL REVOLUTION
1750–1850

THE INDUSTRIAL REVOLUTION
1750–1850
AN INTRODUCTORY ESSAY

H. L. BEALES

*(Late Reader in Economic History
in the University of London)*

FRANK CASS & CO. LTD.
LONDON
1958

First published 1928 for W.E.A.
by Longmans, Green & Co. Ltd.

PRINTED IN GREAT BRITAIN BY
EBENEZER BAYLIS AND SON, LTD., THE
TRINITY PRESS, WORCESTER AND LONDON

CONTENTS

PREFACE TO FIRST EDITION

THE substance and form of this essay have been prompted by the questionings of my fellow-students in Tutorial classes. There lecture and discussion are complementary—gaps in the one are filled in in the other. I have written in the hope that these brief chapters may serve not as a collection of verdicts but as a series of starting-points for group-discussion. Sins of omission and commission may then be overlooked, for the complexity of the subject and the difficulty of anything like finality of interpretation will soon become apparent.

A chapter in *Tristram Shandy* ends thus: "The reader will be content to wait for a full explanation of these matters till the next year—when a series of things will be laid open which he little expects." That sentence might well serve as a standing motto for students and those who try to guide them. It is certainly appropriate in the preface of any book, whether long or short, on the Industrial Revolution.

H. L. BEALES

INTRODUCTION TO NEW EDITION

I HAVE been reluctant to reprint this introductory essay on early industrialization in Britain. The developments of scholarship in a generation of historical study have been so great that it is impossible to incorporate them, even in outline, in a short book. More than that. Pressing needs in the shaping of our public policies, economic and social, internal and external, in this our own day have called for the re-examination of historical experience in new ways. It is idle for historians to declare that they write their histories in a scientific vacuum. They cannot so do. Their very interests have emerged, as curiosity or imaginative reconstruction, from their own social milieu, or their own involvement in the world of their day. Current price movements which reduce or increase their net income, the ins-and-outs of wars and revolutions, mass migrations and peace settlements, cold wars and the rising of backward peoples against crumbling imperialisms, above all, perhaps the restless technical transformation of the productive equipment of their own and other societies with their resultant new living habits, new wealth, new status and ambitions, all over the world . . . these things and others make the cloistered scholarship of any recent history impossible, however sheltered its would-be exponents may seem to be. My quotation from *Tristram Shandy* in 1928 still stands, then, as a necessary foreword.

The varying interpretations of early industrialization in this country have had this present-mindedness in greater or less degree. In the early years of the present century the writings of Mr. and Mrs. Hammond were attuned to the radicalism of the early twentieth century; Sir John Clapham wrote in the context of post-war uncertainties when sturdy individualism was postulating the certainty of collapse if

wicked socialists got their head; Professor Ashton carried
the full armoury of the twentieth-century Ricardian, sym-
pathies and liberalism included but not the labour theory
of value, to the further refinement of the anti-socialist
interpretation of economic expansion. Professor Ashton's
version of the shaping of early industrialization is em-
bedded in his pursuit of quantitative evidence, and Professor
Rostow goes on providing still more of it in increasing
volume up to the moment of our "take-off into self-sustain-
ing growth". And now "economic growth" is a major
interest of economists everywhere . . . and perhaps there are
lessons to be made available by their studies for the guidance
of "backward" or "underdeveloped" economies wherever
they may be found. Present-mindedness, in fact, is normal
. . . and economic history gains, perhaps, more from it than
do other historical specialisms.

The student may well examine one or more of the following, in order to establish contact with this latest phase of
the historiography of industrialization:—

Sir J. Clapham, *An Economic History of Modern Britain*,
Vol. 1 *The Early Railway Age* (1820–50), first published in
1926. He may care to notice that Clapham does not employ
the term "industrial revolution".

T. S. Ashton, *The Industrial Revolution* (1760–1830). This
excellent synthesis in the Home University Library, is the
established starting point for the present day. The same
author's *An Economic History of England: the Eighteenth
Century* (1955) gives his matured analysis of early industrialism up to 1800 but is necessarily narrower than his
brilliant synthesis of seven years before.

The writings of W. W. Rostow, to which reference is made
above, are his *British Economy of the Nineteenth Century*
(1948), and his *Process of Economic Growth* (1953). Further
studies will be forthcoming, which in part are anticipated by
the two large volumes on the *Growth and Fluctuations of the
British Economy*, 1790–1850 (1953) by A. D. Gayer, W. W.
Rostow and Anna J. Schwartz. Colin Clark has revised

and rewritten his *Conditions of Economic Progress* (1951). A most welcome economist's attempt to look at history with fresh eyes is W. A. Lewis, *The Theory of Economic Growth*, while W. H. B. Court, *A Concise Economic History of Britain, from 1750 to Recent Times* (1954) is valuable in itself; and as historians' rather than economists' history, it contains much that is not perceived or differently valued by those who seek to underwrite a theory, old or new, rather than to answer the historian's questions, "what happened and what differences ensued?"

In 1928 I was much more positive than I am now of the power of economic history to unlock the meanings of past experience. I would still defend it as equally valid for this purpose with other historical specialisms. That misleading term "general history" is often currently used, in contrast to "economic history", as a pursuit that has some prior claim to the student's obligatory attention. But the so-called "general" histories are usually little or no more than political histories: such a claim is specious—as specious as the economic historian's claim, if and when made—to any similar precedence. Economic history is valuable as a study which brings past and present usefully together just in proportion as it looks outside its own strict and narrow province. Hence the particular kind of supplement I have made to this old essay, which had to be so embarrassingly brief because of the dimensions and purpose of the series in which it appeared. It is firstly, bibliographical: what shall I advise the student of today to read in order to enable him to discover, as quickly as may be, the meaning of that historical experience which is still, however clumsily, labelled the Industrial Revolution? And secondly, interpretational, especially in social terms: how did this early industrialization emerge out of its social milieu, with what sort of consequences for the ways in which people lived, and what sort of civilization did it produce? One of the outstanding weaknesses of the earlier versions of the history of economic expansion in the reign of George III was its narrow basis. It told the story far too much in "heroic" terms—the omni-competent James Watt, the ingenious Murdoch, the morose but brilliant Crompton, the infinitely persevering and ingenious George Stephenson, and all the other self-help characters of Samuel Smiles's mythology. *The Harvard Research Centre in Entrepreneurial History* has made all that look the naïveté that it was—a mid-Victorian conditioning of the juvenile mentalities, of all ages, which had to be won to the acceptance of the masterful leadership of the great men of the new civilization. Yet even then the limitations of that civilization, and the problems of its architects, are all too often visible. An example will serve to illustrate the masterfulness and the problems. *The Times* had an engaging habit in mid-Victorian days of re-printing its annual summaries of the major events of the year. On the final page of the collection of summaries for the quarter century from the Great Exhibition (1851 to 1875), there appears the following advertisement of the new Walter Press:

"This volume of 598 pages has been set in type by four lads, working at two composing machines, in ten days of eight hours, at the rate of 2,150 lines per day. It has been printed from stereotype plates, in perfected sheets, each containing 128 pages, at the rate of 12,000 per hour on the Walter Press."

What can have been the thought of an elderly compositor who read these words? Or of his trade union? Or of firms with obsolescent presses? The history of the press, from which, as from Crompton's mule, issues a standardized mass-produced merchandise, would be as good as any other industry to illustrate the entrepreneurial progress of industrial civilizations. And the mass-production of the annual summaries of *The Times* by the agency of new machines, illustrates adequately the economic opportunities open to the entrepreneur aware of the spread of literacy. In the course of the remainder of the present century enterprising publishers will rise similarly to the supply of world markets for several hundred millions of newly literate readers. This small example reminds us that social and political as well as economic factors will again shape, or rather go on continuously shaping the development of civilizations, until we see that the history of industrialization is the history of integration—the unification of the single society like that of Great Britain, the knitting together of integrated and multiform societies in an enlarging economic whole or world economy, even *The Crumbling of Empires* (1938) of which Moritz Bonn wrote impressively years ago.

That sort of history won't go into the Smiles mythology, but the Smiles mythology had its usefulness in the mid-Victorian decades. Narrow versions of "the inventor", we know, are not more than individually revealing. "The inventor", is a useful historical category, but innovation, like invention, calls for social as well as economic analysis. The inventor's contribution can be studied in a multitude of recent examples in J. Jewkes, D. Sawers and R. Stillerman, *The Sources of Invention* (1958), but a more interesting approach to historical experience is that of S. C. Gilfilan *The Sociology of Invention* (Chicago, 1935), and essays by Gilfillan and others in *Technological Trends and National Policy* (U.S. Government, Washington, 1937).

In early industrialism the ultimate job of the entrepreneur was to deliver to the daily use of mankind, by economic innovation, the applications of the new sciences embodied in new business units with new forms of internal and external organization, financial and commercial as well as industrial. Space and time had to be subjected to man's will to produce: food, shelter, clothing had to issue from the processes of this subjection. We had ultimately to get from Brindley to Marconi, from road and canal communication to aircraft and telecommunication, from earth to the planets. We had to understand minds as well as to stimulate them to new interests and to subject them to new disciplines. How much quicker and further we would have got, if the early enthusiastic search of ordinary working folk for the means of understanding the scientific bases of new manufacturing practices had been adequately realized. The study of the early history of Mechanics' Institutes, in Dr. Mabel Tylecote, *The Mechanics' Institutes of Lancashire and Yorkshire before 1851* (1957), or Mr. Thomas Kelly, *George Birkbeck* (1957) shows what "good will" was there to be harnessed, and how it came to be too often dissipated can be inferred from a short passage from Charles Babbage's *Economy of Manufactures* (1832):

"A most erroneous and unfortunate opinion prevails among workmen in many manufacturing countries, that their own interest and that of their employers are at variance. The consequences are that valuable machinery is sometimes neglected and then privately injured—that new improvements introduced by the masters, do not receive a fair trial—and that the talents and observations of the workmen are not directed to the improvement of the processes in which they are employed.

"It would be of great importance if in every large establishment the modes of payment could be so arranged that every person employed should derive advantage from the success of the whole and that the profits of each individual should advance as the factory itself produced profit, without the necessity of making any change in the wages agreed upon. This being done, the workmen and capitalist would so shade into each other—would so evidently have a common interest, and their difficulties and distresses would be so mutually well understood that instead of combining to oppress one another, the only combination which could exist would be a most powerful union between both parties to overcome their common difficulties".

Babbage's book was striking. He saw the difficulties of both masters and men; that these difficulties necessitated new harmonies as well as new disciplines, new incentives (as we call them) as well as the older pressures; and that these new incentives would necessitate a re-definition of function and responsibility between man and the machine (labour-saving in a vertical sense), as well as between man and man, or process and process (or the saving of labour horizontally, the product being the assembly of parallel and successive stages of work, as in Adam Smith's famous example of the making of pins). He saw, too, the fear of employers that their workers might secure too large a share of the profit, hence his proposal of co-partnership and profit-sharing in which as in so much else his vision was more penetrating than that of his contemporaries.

Babbage's work gives occasion for thought about industrialization and labour as a whole. That thought may be pursued in all sorts of places. Wilbert E. Moore, *Industrialization and Labour* (1951), though concerned primarily with the ways in which non-industrial civilizations are now being transformed through the influence of the factory on older social forms in such countries as South Africa, India, Mexico and the Far East, discusses the transition to industrialism in ways that cannot but be suggestive to historical students. But we have abundant raw materials of our own, the examination of which informed a valuable Chinese study by H. D. Fong, *Triumph of Factory System in England* (1930) of which there is still no English edition. Its concern is primarily with 1840 onwards, which dating shows how absurd the thought of terminal dates for the "industrial revolution" really is. In the light of the findings of such books, and of a host of publications by the Harvard Entrepreneurial group and, of articles in periodicals national and local in this and other countries, we can now jettison for most purposes most of the secondary books of yesterday. Witt Bowden, *Industrial Society in England Towards the End of the Eighteenth Century* (1925) is still worth while and the careful and illuminating detail of P. Mantoux, *The Industrial Revolution in the Eighteenth Century* (revised edition, 1928) along with Alfred Marshall's *Industry and Trade* (1919) casts much illumination on the whole field of industrial practice and organization. My own advice (not to examinees, of course) is "go straight to the best recent work" and in that I would include the various essays in William Millar (Editor) *Men in Business* (1952) which is international in its fields of study and "social" in its general outlook. L. H. Jenks, *The Migration of British Capital* (1927), deals with British foreign investment up to the startling break of 1875 with so human and broad a grasp of the most attractively varied material as to be one of the major illuminations of the post-Waterloo years. The increasing mobility of all the factors of production was the necessary condition of industrial expansion. We may get answers to some of our questionings in the valuable findings of A. Redford, *Labour Migration in England, 1800–50* (1926) and any of the later books on external migration, e.g. Marcus Lee Hansen, *The Atlantic Migration, 1607–1860* (1945) and N. H. Carrier and J. R. Jeffery, *External Migration, A study of the Available Statistics, 1815–1950* (1953, Her Majesty's Stationery Office). But what we require is not merely topographical or statistical studies. Functional migrational history would be much more illuminating.

It would be easy to compile a formidable list of most useful books on migrational topics. Brinley Thomas, *Migration and Economic Growth* (1954) quickly suggests itself as arising out of economists' current interests and embodying new material of much value. But the time has come to ask for studies of labour which examine it in relation to mechanization over a wide range of industries, to the general history of occupational change socially as well as economically considered, and considered also in terms of adaptation to new capital formation through the modification of skills, the needs of new developments of apprenticeship and of new labour relationships. Consider our curious experience in this present phase of economic tension. There are daily exhortations of politicians to avoid spending, or making wage claims, and to reduce profits. We hear daily fulminations of trade union leadership against the theoretical rectitudes of Cohen Committees, and

there seems to be no possibility of finding a common outlook on wage policy at the top or the bottom even of the
labour movement, industrial or political. Who knows what
should be the functions of trade unionism in the so-called
welfare state or the key to the considerable puzzle of a
heavy trade union vote for the Tories, and other phenomena
equally or more "unhistorical"? That admirably sceptical
and irreverent study of *The Social Foundations of Wages
Policy* (1955) by Barbara Wooton becomes necessary reading
for the student of the pre-Victorian phase of industrialism.
Reading it he will acquire perspective in reverse and get a
deeper awareness than ordinary secondary reconstructions
will stimulate of the difficulties of the transition from a long-
period status system to a weekly contract system of employment. An ingenious Swedish scholar, G. Langenfelt, in
The Historic Origin of the Eight Hours Day (1954, *Stock-
holm*) recalls Robert Owen's statement, as early as 1817,
that grown-up workers should not work more than eight
hours a day and proceeds to find verification of the ancient
English tradition that it was Alfred the Great in the ninth
century who first divided the day into three equal parts for
work, sleep and recreation respectively. "Eight hours work,
eight hours play, eight hours sleep and eight bob a day"
was a common workers' slogan in the pre-1914 years of
this century. There is little enough in the history of wages,
or of the development of occupations, in the general history
of industrial employment, that will go into the quantitative
terms of statistical series. Such series have a delusive
finality which is often wildly unhistorical because concealing
more than they reveal. In any decade of the industrial cycle,
the wage figures must be associated with varying ranges and
intensities of truck payment, varying degrees of mechanization, varying degrees of capital and labour obsolescence,
varying qualities of "welfare capitalism" (or the reverse),
varying survivals of frame rents or their equivalent, varying
elements of security and insecurity. The woolcombers disappeared in their grim competition with machines—ageing

drudges despised by their children in their own households. And how can one assess the real wages of the 40,000 entrants who each week, for better or worse, got sucked into Manchester in the 1840s? Let the open-minded reader consider this passage of a writer in the *Edinburgh Review* of 1813:

"The lower orders . . . have still less good fortune (than the higher and more instructed orders of society) to reckon on. In the whole history of the species there was nothing at all comparable to the improvement of England within the last century; never anywhere was there such an increase of wealth and luxury—so many admirable inventions in the arts—so many works of learning and ingenuity—such a progress in cultivation—such an enlargement of commerce —and yet, in that century, the number of paupers in England had increased fourfold, and is now rated at one-tenth of her whole population, and notwithstanding the enormous sums that are levied and given privately for their relief, and the multitudes that are drained off by the waste of war, the peace of the country is perpetually threatened by the outrages of famishing multitudes". The writer may well have had in mind as he wrote the Gordon Riots of 1780, and a little way ahead lay the agrarian hangings of 1816, the Pentrich (1817) and Peterloo (1819) 'revolutions' and the last Labourers' Revolt (1830). He was arguing against the tenability of any theory of human perfectibility, or law of social progress. "Increasing refinement and ingenuity lead naturally to the establishment of manufactures; and not only enable society to spare a great proportion of its agricultural labourers for this purpose, but actually encourage the breeding of an additional population, to be maintained out of the profits of this new occupation. For a time, too, this answers: and the artisan shares in the conveniences to which his labours have contributed to give birth. But it is in the very nature of the manufacturing system, to be liable to great fluctuation, occasional check and possible destruction; and at all events it has a tendency to produce a greater population than it can permanently support in comfort or prosperity. The average rate of wages, for the last forty years, has been insufficient to maintain a labourer with a tolerably large family; and yet such have been the occasional fluctuations and such the sanguine calculations of persons incapable of taking a comprehensive view of the whole, that the manufacturing population has been prodigiously increased in the same period. It is the interest of the manufacturer to keep this population in excess, as the only sure means of keeping wages low, and wherever the means of subsistence are uncertain, and liable to variation, it seems to be the general law of our nature, that the population should be adapted to the highest, and not to the average rate of supply . . .' Thus, the increase of industry and refinement converts peasants into manufacturers and manufacturers into paupers, "while the chance of their ever emerging from this system becomes constantly less, the more complete and mature the system is which had originally produced it. When manufacturers are long established, and thoroughly understood, it can always be found that persons possessed of a large capital, can carry them upon lower profits than persons of any other description: and the natural tendency of this system, therefore, is to throw the whole business into the hands of great capitalists, and thus not only to render it next to impossible for a common workman to advance himself into the condition of a master, but to drive from the competition the greater part of those moderate dealers, by whose prosperity alone the general happiness of the nation can be promoted. The state of the operative manufacturers, therefore, seems every day more hopelessly stationary; and that great body of the people, it appears to us, is likely to grow into a fixed and degraded *caste*, out of which no person can hope to escape, who has once been enrolled among its members."

I have not been quoting Marx inadvertently. I have been thinking, I admit, as I transcribed that passage from the fashionable *Edinburgh* in the heyday of its greatness, that it must have been desperately hard to know what was going on in the earlier phase of industrialization. Otherwise, the Edinburgh Reviewer would scarcely have postulated so sharply theories we nowadays ascribe to Marx, Lenin, Stalin and Khrushchev. There really is room for thinking again about the effects of the new mobilities of labour and their embodiment in the nice finalities of statistical tables. You can accept, if you like, all the ingenuities of W. G. Hoffman, *British Industry*, 1700 to 1950 (1955), but the reasons why you should do so for the first part of the period covered are not yet adequate. And in this field of labour history, in particular, our studies are not satisfactorily grounded either in analysis of the different kinds of labour system inherited from the past and still prevalent in the early phases of industrialization, or in descriptions of the extent of labour mobilities in different industries, or in comparisons with other economies.

Perhaps it is not just the habit of riding on my particular hobby-horse which impels me to say that the analysis of the industrial revolution is still made too much in economic terms. When I read, say, Rostow's discussion of "the first take-off—the British Industrial Revolution (1783–1802)" and "the take-off into self sustaining growth", I admire the ingenuity, but ask questions which will seem to be irrelevant to the purist in economic history. For example, the dependent economy of Ireland, with its political and religious subservience and its depressing absenteeism (skilfully but unconvincingly explained away by some of the classical economists), and the reconstruction of the Scottish agrarian economy by crofter "clearances" from the Highland Estates of the high nobility left behind them legacies of pauper emigration, indentured labour, disturbed labour supplies, and disturbing participation in labour agitations, and friction which deepened the fluctuations which seemed, in the short run, to threaten the stability of the incipient industrialism. The growing "evil" of the old Poor Law, against which the Malthusians thundered and for which they devised the inhumanities of the new Poor Law of 1834, may well have worn a different face in a new industrial Manchester from that which shone all too clear in the stark ministrations of the new rural Guardians. That great manufacturer, John Kennedy, a most humane cotton lord, and much more alert to the true character of change than contemporaries (like Ure, Nassau, Senior and Cooke Taylor) who paid flying visits to factories and found them well-nigh models of perfection, may be heard on this bunch of characteristics of the new industrialism:

"Under the worst circumstances that can befall the English poor, they have still a parish to look to for support, and they seldom think of exchanging the mode of relief which is thus afforded for the precarious subsistence of vagrant begging. Parochial relief is a certain provision, which, when well administered, becomes a stimulus to a degree of industry in the lower classes which we never find in countries destitute of such regulations. The happy effects of this incitement on their minds are, so far as I have observed, apparent in preventing their spirit of activity from drooping or being broken down. But whenever the lower orders are reduced, as in other countries, to the extreme limit at which existence can be maintained, then, if unsupported, their energy entirely fails them; degradation, both moral and physical, immediately succeeds; and the prospect of restoring them to industry and activity becomes almost hopeless. The evil, however, does not rest with the debasement of the lower class, for this class may not un-aptly be compared to an indispensable part of a moving piece of mechanism, of which, if the form or situation be altered, the whole machine is deranged. Exactly the same thing happens with respect to the different classes con-stituting a nation; for when the lower orders have, by the inefficiency of their exertions, lost all incitement to activity, the progress of general improvement receives an immediate check, which it may require centuries to counteract . . .

"Among the lower orders it may, I think, be safely

affirmed, that industry can only be found, where artificial wants have crept in, and have acquired the character of necessaries. In England especially the greater energy of the lower rank is mainly to be attributed to that superiority in respect to domestic comforts, which they possess over those of the two sister countries; comforts, which, having once enjoyed, they will never resign, whilst industry and activity can secure their continuance. Englishmen of the lower order, when scarcity visits the land, or when calamity in trade occurs of sufficient extent to deprive them of the power of subsisting by means of their own industry, fall back upon the poor-rate. By this they are relieved, until the cause of their depression is removed. The elasticity of their minds is thus preserved and their spirits remain unbroken. In such cases relief is generally administered, according to the wants of the several applicants, by the most respectable and conscientious individuals of the middle class, who, while their sympathy is sufficiently awakened, are restrained from inconsiderate or lavish bounty, by consequences in which they themselves must participate. This kind of relief, it appears to me, has not a natural or direct tendency to debase those to whom it is extended; for the poor-rate is to them a capital indirectly arising out of their own former labour, and upon this capital they have a claim, until, by the revival of trade, their industry and activity are again called forth unimpaired. Whilst preferring such a claim, no individual can possibly entertain a feeling of degradation; but, on the other hand, no one can feel otherwise than de-based who is compelled, by the short-sighted policy of the higher classes of society, to solicit alms as a vagrant beggar.

"An opinion has been maintained by a political economist of great and deserved celebrity, that want and misery operate as checks to early marriages. This opinion appears to me to be ill-founded; for prudential restraint exists, I believe, only where a certain degree of comfort and luxury is enjoyed, and where the sacrifice of those comforts must be the inevitable consequence of an indiscreet marriage. On the principle assumed by Mr. Malthus, that the means of subsistence regulate the amount of population, without any reference to the habits of the people, the population of England, where there is comparatively little misery, ought to bear a much greater proportion to its extent than that of Scotland or Ireland, where this supposed check to natural increase exists in a far greater degree. The fact, however, is otherwise. And in those countries the real increase is even much greater than it appears, on account of the constant emigration into other countries where a better subsistence may be procured.

"In England, the lower classes now form a community of no small consideration in the state. They are great consumers both of the produce and of the manufactures of the country, and having acquired a taste for domestic comforts, and even for a degree of luxury, their wants have established a home demand, superior in its extent to the market afforded by all the world besides. It cannot, however, be said of the English poor that they have eaten the bread of idleness; for had that been the case this country never could have attained its present state of wealth and comfort. Great wealth can only be accumulated where great industry prevails; and the superior opulence of the middle rank in England furnishes, in my view, a complete answer to the arguments against the poor laws. By those laws the lower orders have been prevented, under adverse circumstances, from falling into that lethargy so fatal to industry, which seems to have seized the people of other countries, where no adequate provision is made for the indigent. And the energy thus excited and cherished has amply repaid the middle and higher classes, by extending itself to them, and even to the government of the country."

This long quotation has been made both to draw attention to contemporary writing which is not much used in our current historiography and to support my plea for much fuller consideration of the social factors which conditioned economic change in the pre-Victorian period.

It would go too far afield for this introduction to attempt the barest outline of the social history of English industrialism in its early phase. Fortunately we have one book which does set us on our feet. It is a neglected book, and being about Scotland it will (I guess) continue to be neglected in England. It is L. J. Saunders, *Scottish Democracy, 1815–40* (1950). Planned as the first of two volumes, the work is left sadly incomplete by its author's death, but even so its analysis of rural and urban change, land monopoly, of poverty, philanthropy and educational expansion (in universities and professions) is mature and convincing. If that is read, and to it is added such other work as F. C. Lane and J. C. Riemersma, *Enterprise and Social Change* (1953), G. D. H. Cole, *Studies in Class Structure* (1955), E. Hughes, *North Country Life in the Eighteenth Century* (1952), D. Marshall, *English People in the Eighteenth Century* (1956) and the steady flow of new histories of hitherto neglected industries, such as L. F. Haber, *The Chemical Industry during the Nineteenth Century* (1958), studies of obsolescent financial organizations such as L. S. Pressnell, *Country Banking in the Industrial Revolution* (1956) and obsolescent legal and business attitudes as reflected in B. C. Hunt, *The Development of the Business Corporation in England, 1800–67* (Harvard Univ. Press, 1936), there will become apparent many of the tensions and incompatibilities as well as the driving force and modifying catalysts of the new industrialism. That society was witnessing simultaneously the decline in the prestige and influence of a landed aristocracy, its displacement in the leadership of economic enterprise and its transformation by collaboration with a new middle class in the widening range of governmental processes, the expanding outlook on inherited aristocratic monopolies of political power, public administration, local government and judicial administration, an ultimately successful alleviation of the Establishment's strangle-hold on education by such mere infidels and charlatans as dissenting academies, Scottish universities, the brand-new utilitarian University of London, and Chartist agitators, the irresistible definition of a new form of property in the transferable share of the limited liability company, and of newly necessary formulations of opinion in the quarterlies and weeklies which a mechanising press was pouring out, despite the reactionary taxes on knowledge, in increasing clouds . . . But for all this a new synthesis is necessary. It is not easy to get it now that democracy is almost a dirty word. But a first step towards it might well be taken through the reading of Bulwer Lytton (as he became) *England and The English* (1835), with its Appendix by J. S. Mill on *Bentham's Philosophy*. And the growing literature on the seventeenth and eighteenth century aristocracy will acquire thus a witty and discerning footnote, which may well lend it both perspective and point:

> Lord Stafford mines for coal and salt
> The Duke of Norfolk deals in malt;
> The Douglas in red herrings;
> And noble name and cultured land,
> Palace and park, and vassal band,
> Are powerless to the notes of hand
> Of Rothschild or the Barings.

Or, as a forgotten essayist, Sir T. C. Morgan, put it in 1830: "Let people talk as they will of our glorious constitution, the right-minded will be more inclined to celebrate our glorious coal mines. Great Britain is more indebted for all that makes it 'the envy of surrounding nations and the admiration of the world' to Mulciber than Minerva, and Venus was not so much out as some have thought, when she preferred the sooty divinity of Lemnos for a husband, to all the smarter but less serviceable gods of Olympus. The steam-engine, indeed, the latest-born but greatest of the sons of Vesta, has become a fourth estate of the realm, and is fairly worth the other three. It is the vivifying principle of taxation, and is a more powerful conservator of the peace than an army of new police, or a host of vice-suppressing associations. The instant it stops working, the people becomes turbulent and less contented, and when it resumes its activity, the agitator's 'occupation is gone'. The steam-engine is the real and effective balance in the state; it maintains the credit of the national debt, it is the thunderbolt of war, and the fruitful olive of peace . . . Steam-engines are better subjects than men, they have many advantages also over the aristocracy. They never combine to make corn dear; they have no younger children to quarter on the public; nor do they insist upon making their tutors bishops; they never rat for a ribbon, nor sell their country for an empty title. In the hands of Perkins himself, 'with all appliances and means to boot', they indulge not in murderous *battues*, nor do they fortify their preserves with laws which exceed the atrocity of a Draco . . . Steam-engines, when well used, can do no wrong.' But how to use them well? We still have much to learn about that, and our great-grandfathers had even more. If we can establish a reasonable historical perspective, we shall not despair of the present which has arisen out of the past and perhaps (though this is very doubtful) be able to look forward again. After all, every Innovation, even the open mind, has always been dangerous to some one.

April 1958.   H. L. BEALES

CHAPTER I

INTRODUCTORY

CERTAIN ages in the story of civilization stand out so distinctly that historians have devised special distinguishing labels for them. Such labels are mere summarized descriptions of the most prominent feature of these periods. They are never more than superficially adequate. Among these labels is the term "the Industrial Revolution".

Popular usage has established the label "the Industrial Revolution". Like the term "the Reformation", it is a generalized description of a phase of human experience. It is about as good a term as the term "the Reformation" and, it is certainly no better. To try to discredit it now seems pedantic. Yet some economic historians are so dissatisfied with it that they avoid its use. Because of this it is necessary to explain the sense in which it is here employed. In so doing, we shall indicate the scope of this essay, and the reader will be able to decide for himself whether this label is appropriate or not.

It was Arnold Toynbee who gave general currency to the term, "The Industrial Revolution". In 1884, a few months after his death, his lectures on the Industrial and Agrarian Revolution at the end of the eighteenth and the beginning of the nineteenth centuries were given book form. The date of their delivery and publication is significant. The great era of constructive social legislation was just opening. The Labour movement on its political and industrial sides, was beginning to discover its strength and guiding its march towards new and broader horizons. The village labourer was at last at the ballot-box along with his urban colleague. Mid-Victorian complacency was waning. The factory had visibly beaten the domestic workshop. Great wealth and great poverty existed side by side, equally visibly, and many minds were disturbed about it. In all classes of society economic questions were being vigorously discussed. Toynbee's work caught up the new interests of his day— these were his inspiration—and helped towards giving them depth and direction. He surveyed the age of George III and saw great changes in agriculture, industry, trade, population, economic policy and thought. In sum and consequence these changes seemed to his penetrating gaze and sympathetic spirit to make a break with the past. That break seemed clear enough to him to justify the application to it of the word "revolution". The most conspicuous factor in bringing this revolution to birth was the great progress in industry. So he called the epoch "The Industrial Revolution", and showed how the world of his own day was the issue of it.

The term revolution is always disconcerting. Not only does it bear a certain "red" tinge, it suggests also the reversal, and the reversal under extreme pressure, of established usages. However appropriate the term revolution may be in the political field, it seems inappropriate in the economic. The changes which are described as revolutionary rose spontaneously from ordinary economic practice, and they were constructive in that they gave an increased power of satisfying wants. It is impossible, too, to find a beginning or an ending of these developments. The inventions on which rested the enlargement of industrial enterprise established themselves only slowly. New economic ideas, revised economic policies, modified economic relationships, all were shaped gradually. The extended probings of scholars who have followed in Toynbee's trail seem to show that there never was an industrial revolution at all. As Unwin put it: "When, on looking back, we find that the revolution has been going on for two centuries, and had been in preparation for two centuries before that, when we find that both in its causes and its consequences it affects the lot of that three-quarters of the human race who are still farmers and peasants as profoundly as it does that of the industrial worker, we may begin to doubt whether the term Industrial Revolution, though useful enough when it was first adopted, has not by this time served its turn."[1]

This dissatisfaction with Toynbee's label it is easy to echo. If the term "industrial revolution" savours of reproach or condemnation, it is an unhappily chosen epithet for a singularly constructive epoch. If it suggests the sudden and cataclysmic, it is equally unfaithful. If it implies any inevitable association of economic advance with social tribulation and widespread hardship of circumstance, it does prejudge development in an unfortunate way.

Yet one must admit that the age of Doctor Johnson did perish. It is useless to suggest that a vast increase of man's productive power did not occur: the England of the steam-engine and the threshing-machine was not the England of the horse-gin and the flail. The disgusting urban concentrations of the days of Dickens were both vaster and nastier than the pleasant country towns which Defoe found in the cloth-working counties of the south-west. The village labourer of Walpole's day was not the sorry toiler of the great epoch of Queen Victoria. The life of the country had changed: the civilization of Free Trade England was different, different in kind, from the civilization of Farmer George. It may be true that each particular aspect of that change, when examined under the statistician's microscope, shows as a change not of kind but of degree. But the sum of these changes was overwhelming: and the process of adding sum to sum, like the process of compound interest, amounted to a revolution. Analogy is useful to make this point clear. The historical student of Russian development sees much of continuity in the expedients of Bolshevik Russia with those of Czarist Russia: he loses his way if he thinks that one is really like the other. A recent definition of revolution suggests that it is the substitution of one system

[1] G. Unwin, *Studies in Economic History* (ed. R. H. Tawney, 1927), p. 15.

of legality for another. That definition may well be applied in this sphere also. The industrial revolution replaced one social system or one civilization by another. Before it emerged, agriculture provided the economic basis of English life: after it, the basis was industry, extractive and manufacturing. A small population became large: a narrow material equipment was expanded: low standards of consumption were made more lavish: the working classes became articulate. A civilization based on the plough and the pasture perished—in its place stood a new order, resting, perhaps dangerously, on coal, iron and imported textile materials.

The term "industrial revolution" sums up these changes. That there were innovators in the economic field, that there were would-be revolutionaries here as well as in France is true; but there is no need to seek such narrow justifications for the term. Nor does the verbal infelicity in using the word revolution for a long process rather than a short series of events matter very much. It would be mere perversity to suggest that the result of the cycle of events was less than fundamental. Further, what happened here has been reproduced with appropriate variations elsewhere. There have been parallel, if later, "industrial revolutions" in other countries. The comparative study of them shows the same general features whether it is examined in Japan, in the United States, in Germany, in South Africa, in Canada, even in China. There is a phase in the economic and social life of many nations so clearly marked as to necessitate some descriptive term. The term "industrial revolution" draws attention to a very important aspect of it.

One other point may be made in explanation of the continued use of the term "industrial revolution". It is sometimes maintained that a quantitative examination of the leading features of the period of so-called revolution tones down the high colours and produces a softened picture. This may well be true. Both the achievements and the miseries have been exaggerated. Particularly, it would seem,

the social historian, as Dr. Clapham complains,[1] has un-
duly neglected the statistics of wages and prices, of trade
movements and population, so frequent in parliamentary
papers and elsewhere. Such neglect has perpetuated legends
—for instance, "the legend that everything was getting worse
for the working man down to some unspecified date
between the drafting of the People's Charter and the Great
Exhibition". But if it is argued that the social and economic
changes of the industrial revolution were in any final sense
changes merely of degree and not of form, changes of
quantity not of quality, one must dissent. There are changes
in the quality of life which statistics do not reveal. It is
here contended that such changes did take place in the
period of our study. Even Harriet Martineau, unswerving
apologist for the new industrialism and for "the great
natural laws of society" whose operation seemed so un-
natural to working-men, admitted them.[2] They are analysed
in a profoundly moving way in Dr. Gaskell's study of the
changes wrought in the social structure by the use of
steam machinery.[3] The recognition of their fundamental
character produced such different manifestations as
Disraeli's *Sybil* (1845) and Karl Marx's *Capital*. Disraeli
sought to build a new and better Jerusalem on "Young
England" Toryism, which would reunite the two Englands
of rich and poor by developing a protecting benevolence in
the one and a spirit of trust and obedience in the other. Karl
Marx, on the other hand, looked to revolution as the final
issue. Yet both were reading the same blue-books for
descriptions of the social system which had come into being.

Perhaps an analogy will make the point clear for those
who are disinclined to accept the fundamental character of
the Industrial Revolution. In earlier days in this country

[1] J. H. Clapham, *An Economic History of Modern Britain* (1926),
Preface, p. vii.

[2] See, for example, *History of the Thirty Years' Peace* (1849),
Vol. IV, chap. 5.

[3] See *The Manufacturing Population of England* (1833), and *Artisans
and Machinery* (1836).

local famines were distressingly frequent: in recent centuries they have disappeared. There were markets and dealers and communications then as now. Statistics would show an enlargement of their functions, even perhaps a replacement of forestallers and regraters by "constructive" speculators. But we are justified in saying that a change in the quality of our common life has been effected when we are no longer at the mercy of famine, even if the statistics limp behind the facts. So with the industrial revolution. The working-class student has learnt to believe that in the century of achievement and stress lying between (approximately) 1750 and 1850 he may find the root of his present-day problems and aspirations. It is impossible to deny that he is right.

CHAPTER II

THE CRADLE OF THE INDUSTRIAL REVOLUTION

NAPOLEON spoke of China as a giant asleep, and added, "when he wakes up he will move the world". The same thing might have been said of Russia in the seventeenth century. Czar Peter the Great (1672–1725) made up his mind that Russia should wake up, and, under his leadership, play the part of giant refreshed. He realized that he would have to put his country to school and the only possible schoolmaster was Western Europe. He set himself the task, first, of discovering the secrets of Western efficiency and then of introducing their practice in his own country. With that aim he made a journey to Western Europe in 1697. He was so willing to learn that he resided, at times, in mean lodgings and even worked as a ship's carpenter. He was especially energetic in his study of the shipyards and industrial technique of Holland and England. He inspected factories, workshops, hospitals, educational institutions and military and industrial establishments in Holland; in England, he visited the rooms of the Royal Society of Arts, lodged near the King's Wharf, Deptford, made excursions to London, Oxford, Woolwich and Portsmouth, saw the Tower ("wherein", his journal stated, "it is customary to lodge the more honourable men of England"), the Mint, and the House of Lords. "His whole impression, as derived from his fifteen months' tour, must have been a noisy, vast, smoky vista of factories, foundries, shipyards, wharves and machinery".[1]

So far as it goes, Peter the Great's impression of England was true enough. But there were other phases of our economic life which he did not see. The major activity of the country was still to be found in agriculture, and though

[1] See account in Kluchevsky, *A History of Russia*, Vol. IV, pp. 20–23.

shipbuilding and cannon-founding, as the Czar saw them, were highly organized capitalistic industries, it was generally held that our chief manufacture was that of woollen cloths. Defoe even insisted that it was "the greatest single manufacture" in the world. In other respects, too, Peter's view would be incomplete. He could scarcely be expected to appreciate the extent to which London and the southern counties led the northern counties in wealth and numbers. Yet in so far as he saw here a hive of progressive industry, shaping a pre-eminence to which each succeeding generation was to add, he saw what actually was. The Industrial Revolution did not, in fact, develop in an unlikely place. On the contrary, even a cursory examination of the prevailing economic structure and tendencies reveals a laboratory of resourceful experiment and an environment singularly favourable to the extension of industrial enterprise into fresh fields.

A bird's-eye view of the economic order of the eighteenth century must begin with agriculture. Our farmers were able to supply the nation with food, and frequently to have a surplus for export. A bigger wool production could have been absorbed because our cloths were successful in foreign markets, but the yield of our pastures was good. Despite the convulsions of the preceding century much water-logged land had been reclaimed by ambitious drainage schemes and many publications bear witness to a significant willingness to experiment with new crops, such as clover, the potato and the turnip. It perhaps made for technical progressiveness that land changed hands pretty readily in this country. The Civil War had been financed in part by the sequestration of royalist estates. While this process gave opening to the sinister activities of the land-speculator, it did mean that fresh capital was made available for agrarian development, for the new landowners were those who had been successful in commerce. "I dare oblige myself," wrote Defoe, "to name five hundred great estates, within one hundred miles of London, which within eighty years past, were the possessions of the ancient English Gentry, which are now bought up, and in the possession of Citizens and Tradesmen, purchased fairly by money raised in trade."[1] Such people were not, as landlords, likely to be sympathetic towards established customs: rack-rents and enclosures would seem reasonable expedients: their new grandeur would easily express itself in the laying out of elaborate parks. The forces of resistance to change were not negligible, of course, but the rate of change, and its spread, depend on such economic circumstances as humbler folk cannot control. A recently discovered tract of 1691 by Richard Baxter shows that hard times had come to the small rent-paying farmer in the later seventeenth century: his lot was worse than that of artisans, household servants, or even his own labourers, and he was helpless to improve it because he was "servilely dependent" on his landlord. He had little of either capital or knowledge: his land was in the open fields: the downward tendency of corn prices was against him. Thus economic circumstance was moving towards the great enclosures which drove him from his comfortless holding and made of his children the "new proletariat of textile workers which is to be found in the suburbs of London, in the clothing districts of the West, and in South-East Lancashire, in the first half of the eighteenth century."[2] The later system of capital landlord, tenant farmer and landless labourer was already taking shape, though its more rapid spread was delayed by the peace and prosperity of Walpole's era. With its growth the labourer had to choose between land and manufacture as the source of his livelihood. The worker who combined both was steadily disappearing.

In industry there is the same movement towards a new economic order. There were some, it is true, who in the absence of exact information believed that our manufactures were declining in the early eighteenth century, but no important evidence supported their pessimism. Indeed,

[1] *A Plan of the English Commerce* (1728), pp. 83–84.
[2] G. Unwin, *Studies in Economic History* (1927), p. 351.

the great industrial towns of the future were already fore-shadowed, if dimly. "Let the curious," wrote Defoe, "examine the great Towns of Manchester, Warrington, Macclesfield, Halifax, Leeds, Wakefield, Sheffield, Birmingham, Frome, Taunton, Tiverton and many others. Some of these are mere villages; the highest magistrate in them is a constable, and few or no families of gentry among them; yet they are full of wealth, and full of people, and daily increasing in both. . . . Let the curious enquirer travel a little farther, and look into the countries adjacent to these towns, and there they will see the villages stand thick, the market towns not only more in number, but larger, and fuller of inhabitants; and in short, the whole country full of little end-ships or hamlets, and scattered houses, that it looks all like a planted colony, everywhere full of People, and the people everywhere full of business." If it was thus in the manufacturing areas, in agricultural districts it was the reverse. "The manufacturing counties are calculated for business, the unemployed counties for pleasure; the first are thronged with villages and great towns, the last with parks and great forests; the first are stored with people, the last with game; the first are rich and fertile, the last waste and barren; the diligent part of the people are fled to the first, the idler part are left at the last; the first eat the fat and the kernel of all, and enjoy the soft, being by their diligence made able to buy it; and the last eat the husk, the coarse and the hard; pinch, and live miserable, being without employment, except mere drudging and consequently without money."[1]

The age-long rivalry of town and country was coming to a head, and the future lay with those localities whence "the fat and the kernel and the soft" could be won. Whilst industry was still dispersed, it was dispersed in recognizable areas, and these areas were being knit more closely together round their metropolitan centre. Further, the battle against industrial monopolies had been fought and won in the

[1] *Plan of the English Commerce* (1728), pp. 84–90.

struggle with the Stuarts. Free competition in manufacture had been established save for gild survivals and the inventor's patent, which latter was highly unpopular. The religious disabilities of nonconformists had driven them to seek habitations where they would be free from the obnoxious Corporation and Test Acts and other statutes against dissenters. Thus such towns as Birmingham and Manchester attracted a virile population forced by circumstance to habits of opportunism.

Industries in the pre-factory era showed considerable diversity of organization. Factories, large workshops, the small domestic workshop housing a semi-independent worker and his working family, all existed side by side. The factory was not yet the usual industrial unit; nor, on the other hand, was the independent producer or the part-time manufacturer the representative figure of English industry. Relationships essentially capitalistic characterized English industry before the industrial revolution developed. Such a statement need occasion no surprise if it be recalled that in the seventeenth century, with grants of monopoly as basis, full-blown industrial capitalism had taken shape in a number of industries.[1] After the passing of monopoly, the commanding figure in the industrial field was the merchant, who added resources of capital to his command of the market. Businesses of all sorts show an elaborate network of middlemen upon whom that humbler figure, the manufacturer, was dependent. The future "captain of industry", save in exceptional cases, was as yet no more than a noncommissioned officer in the army of production. He commanded only slender resources and worked to the merchants' orders. He received his raw materials from one who in essentials was an employer; he might or might not engage journeymen and apprentices to assist in his own workshop, or to labour, through him as intermediary, in their own

[1] This subject is summarized in the earlier chapters of H. Levy, *Monopoly and Competition* (new edition, 1928, entitled *Monopolies, Cartels and Trusts in British Industry*).

homes: in some cases he might work for himself in the intervals of work for another. Considerable variation in manufacturing arrangements was possible, but the field of industry was no longer, if it ever had been, occupied by independent producers to any large extent. The wage relationship was well-nigh universal. Coming changes cast their shadow unmistakably in 1732. In that year half a dozen Stockport manufacturers acquired a mill and started a silk manufacture. Their impulse came from the purchase by Parliament of Lombe's silk-throwing machinery when his patent expired in that year. Parliament took that step for the purpose of stimulating manufacturers to adopt Lombe's machinery, and Lombe's machinery, pirated from Italy, was capable of use only in a factory. It had made a great impression with its 26,586 wheels, its 97,746 movements and its water-wheel of 24 feet diameter revolving three times a minute. Hence the Stockport reproduction of the Derby silk-throwing factory "marks an epoch in the rise of the Factory System."[1] What Defoe as early as 1728 called the "revolution in trade" was leading directly to that type of industrial organization which was to supplant all rivals. Its complete victory merely awaited the conjunction of favourable circumstances.

Trading and manufacturing enterprise were still in protectionist leading-strings. The effectiveness of the authoritative regulation of economic activity by the state may have varied at different epochs but its scope was wide at all times. A system or policy which appealed to the statesman seeking revenue, to the fervent nationalist intent on his country's strength against equally aggressive rivals, and to the vested interests whose pursuit of private advantage seemed to reconcile the service of mammon and the state, was not likely to pass without a struggle. It is true that it was more liberal, or less illiberal, at some times than at others; that it was, in fact, a tendency of thought rather than a system. But it would be hazardous to suggest that it

[1] G. Unwin, *Samual Oldknow and the Arkwrights* (1924), p. 23.

made any very important contribution to economic progress in the eighteenth century, or that it greatly impeded it. The volume of imports and exports increased fivefold in the course of the century, an increase for which neither the mercantilist devices of the politician nor the schemings of the merchant to get his aid can be held responsible. Yet even in economic policy signs of change had appeared. Some habits of regulation were rapidly becoming obsolete, notably the statutory fixing of wages and the enforcement of old standards of manufacture. Walpole showed elasticity as well as resourcefulness in his handling of fiscal questions: he purged the tariff of heavy export duties and eased the duties on imported raw materials. If the pressure of war caused a hasty retreat from these liberal tendencies when Walpole's peace era came to an end, their appearance had helped towards the ultimate emergence of those ideas of freedom which Adam Smith was to render articulate.

One other fact may be added to this outline. The needs of war finance had brought into being a national debt, and a Bank of England. The debt and the Bank exercised a great influence on the development of the country. The government borrowed from the Bank, and granted it the right of issuing notes. It acquired a stock of gold which gave it a central position in the financial system of the country. Thus it became the government's bank, and the banker's bank, for its notes were the reserve of other banks in London and the country. It was a century before the country's financial institutions formed a system which was both elastic and reliable, but a clear outline of that system had been sketched in. There was, then, nothing on the financial side permanently to retard progress. It is true that country banks failed disastrously at not infrequent intervals, but the commercial life of England centred in London where the financial system was at its best. Capital resources became available as and when required, and their mobility even in the eighteenth century was an important factor in development.

CHAPTER III

THE AGRARIAN REVOLUTION

THE term "agrarian revolution" has been applied to two phases of the history of English farming, the first in the sixteenth century and the second in George III's reign. These periods show certain points of similarity, the examination of which throws light on the determining factors of agrarian change.

In both periods rising prices and enclosures came together. In the earlier case, the upward climb of prices was due to a flagrant debasement of the coinage and a steady inflow, over a long period, of bullion from the Spanish colonies in the New World: in the later, war conditions brought high expenditure and taxation, blockade, and inflation. In both cases, enclosure was a means by which the landed interest met the altering circumstances, and in both cases it was a means by which technical progress in agriculture was extended. Equally, in both cases, enclosure exercised a profound influence upon social and economic relationships in the countryside. In the earlier period, however, the forces of resistance to change would seem to have been considerably greater than they were in the later. At any rate, the scope of the later enclosure movement was vastly greater than that of the Tudor period, and the destruction of the still extensive common fields was effected with comparative ease. But the use of the term "agrarian revolution" serves to obscure the fact that throughout our rural history, the process of change, of the steady disintegration of the open-field system, has been continuous. What took place in George III's reign, or in Tudor England, was but the intensification of tendencies and influences normally operative. The transformation of serfdom, the building up of a land market, the establishment of improved methods of tillage and pasture-farming to meet the demands of town-dwellers and manufacturers were as much a part of the movement towards capitalistic farming as the enclosures themselves. It was when enclosure coincided with large movements in prices that it seemed, and was, revolutionary.

The comparison between Tudor and Georgian England may reasonably be carried farther. In the earlier period the enclosing landlord's action was to a large extent defensive in aim. The villein had become a free man, having exchanged his customary services for money payments. These, fixed at times of stable prices, represented a diminishing real income to the landlord in times of rising prices. Nobody save the beneficiary likes unearned increments, and landlords were no exception to this rule. When a lease fell in, or a copyhold came up for renewal, the landlord took his chance of improving his position. He raised rents to the highest possible point; he exacted very large fines for the renewal of tenancies; he took land into his own hands, refusing renewals, enclosed it, and then let it at rents which corresponded with prices. It is hard to blame him, but at the same time it is impossible not to recognize that his action seriously disturbed, if it did not uproot, the humbler folk who had resided on his estate. In the later period, the same sort of thing happened, but on a vastly bigger scale, and amid the added complications which sprang from a growing population and a changing industrial system. In the later period, moreover, there was a much more complete disappearance of the "waste" lands of the village: enclosure, that is, was a comprehensive process finally extinguishing the possibility of squatting on unoccupied ground. Circumstances not of the landlord's making added to the small farmer's difficulties. Rising prices had caused his markets to shrink, his main surplus being that of dairy produce and poultry on which people economized; but corn-prices steadily rose, in answer to the demand of increasing numbers as well as from general causes, and corn was the main concern of the larger farmer. The new farming technique was scarcely applicable to the routine of the open-field, and so enclosure was a necessity in the interests of progress. The yield of enclosed lands was greater, the rents and tithes to be gathered therefrom were vastly higher. Hence there was a gathering of circumstances which made the call for enclosure irresistible.

Enclosure to which all parties consented left behind it no recriminations. Enclosure carried out by legal force or sheer force stirred up bitter resentments. In both the periods of agrarian revolution Parliament was sensitive to the prayer, "God speed the plough". In the former, the plough was the main support of the people: husbandry was the means whereby idleness, drunkenness and vice were avoided, and the source from which armies were drawn. Other interests than those of the landed aristocracy were reckoned up, and government did what lay in its power to check the pulling down of houses and the encroachment of sheep-farming on tillage. "The balancing of the misery of the people and the decay of the realm's strength with some abridgement to gentlemen," wrote Cecil, "hath no proportion." In the eighteenth century, in contrast, landed aristocracy was supreme in parliament. As a ruling class, it never doubted that its interests were the nation's interests. There were solid economic arguments in favour of enclosure: the leading agriculturists advocated it. Village Hampdens and rural Miltons were mute as well as inglorious. Enclosure, therefore, was by Act of Parliament. It is true that enclosure awards admitted all who could show recognizable claim to land to a share in its redistribution. But there was no satisfactory means of evaluating common-rights, and a share in the allotment meant a share also in the expenses of enclosure—legal, fencing, road-making. To reconstruct the old village life after enclosure was impossible: to effect a happy adaptation to the new conditions was possible to very few. Enclosure inevitably meant, therefore, the extinction of the village community with its age-long customs and traditions. That the process was forced through at a period when scattered rural industries were being slowly abandoned to the town increased the pain of transition. The enlargement of farms followed, and increase of corn and meat supplies, also, where the newly enclosed land was given up to the new farming methods. But the price which had to be paid for these things was indeed a heavy one.

It is not easy to decide whether that price was worth paying. Enclosures near a large town which provided a good market can scarcely have had catastrophic effects even on those who got only a small allotment. Moreover, it is impossible to know how large the proportion was of common-right cottages—common-rights after all were individual properties —or of those who, by custom but without legal claim, pastured a cow on the waste. Yet when full allowance has been made for the possibility of exaggeration, the landless labouring class must have been enlarged, directly or indirectly, as a result of enclosures, and rural poverty must have been greatly extended by the suppression of non-legal but customary usages of the commons. In 1801 that honest and experienced observer, Arthur Young, still advocated enclosure, but he urged that in all future enclosures a better attention to the needs of the poor was an unmistakable necessity.

"At all times up to the beginning of the nineteenth century," it has been observed, "the agricultural labourer started with an initial, and often hereditary, advantage, in that he had a direct claim to certain privileges attached to the land . . . after the second enclosure movement he lost this advantage, and was placed in equality with those at the bottom of other industries."[1] Those at the bottom of other industries have never been happily placed. To Cobbett as he rode over the countryside the evidence of deterioration was plain to see. He was too good a farmer merely to vituperate enclosure, and too good a countryman to accept

[1] J. A. Venn, *Foundations of Agricultural Economics* (1922), p. 197.

rural poverty as a necessity. He blamed the rapacity of landlords and tax-eaters and tithe-gatherers for what he saw, and he realized that the zeal for enclosure had often been pushed too far. But in truth more than war circumstances had operated to depress the labourer. What had taken place was the final rounding-off of the system of capitalistic farming. The trinity of capitalistic landlord, tenant farmer and landless labourer had been defined. It was a social disaster that the third member of that trinity had lost status as well as comfort.

Enclosure has often been blamed for the extinction of the small landowner. For that, however, it cannot be held responsible. Just when he began finally to disappear is uncertain, but it is clear that economic circumstance was proving too much for him before the enclosing fury of the period of the French wars burst out. Exaggerated ideas of the tendency for the smallholder to disappear have also been common. The census of 1831 showed a very considerable survival. In the agriculture of that day, for each occupying household there were two and a half labouring households. The proletarian element in agriculture, therefore, was not so large a proportion as in industry.[1] But high rents and low resources especially when prices broke after the war, forced farmers to keep wages as low as possible, and to a large degree agricultural employment was the exacting employment of small masters. The difficulty of protective organization was made insuperable by the farm labourer's isolation, social and intellectual, and by the successful attack on the Dorchester labourers. Emigration and suicide were almost synonymous in the earlier decades of the nineteenth century: escape that way was not very tempting. Railway construction and operation brought a new life to many; though not one of opulence, it was less servile and a little better paid. The rising town industries where human beings were accessory to machines absorbed still more.

[1] J. H. Clapham, *An Economic History of Modern Britain* (1926), p. 113.

Rebellion, as in the revolts of 1830–31, brought no relief. The village labourer was compelled to endure prolonged poverty in an environment from which hope had vanished. No class has in the nineteenth century so sombre a history.

What may be set in the balance against this record of poverty? There was positive gain in the enlarged farm and the new agricultural technique. Agricultural experiment had produced some striking and important results. The Norfolk pioneers had discovered a rotation of crops which had cut out the necessity of fallows and provided a winter feed for cattle. More cattle meant more manure: more manure meant bigger crops: bigger crops meant more profit: more profit meant higher rents and better living. Bakewell and the Collings did for the raising of cattle and sheep what Tull and Townshend had done for tillage. Arthur Young popularized the new knowledge till scientific agriculture became a not uncommon enthusiasm—a word synonymous with fanaticism in the eighteenth century. But it spread slowly especially among small farmers and on heavy soils. As yet it was very tentative, being based on trial and error rather than science, and was more appropriate to large farms than small. The capital outlay and greater labour costs barred its use among poor farmers; and in the open fields, though farming was by this time individualistic, the fallow was still generally retained. The full triumph of the new farming awaited adequate farm machinery and the passing of the post-war depression. The former came only when light engineering had made significant progress, though Cobbett found steam-threshing in the northern counties, and the devoted followers of Captain Swing demolished simpler threshing-machines in the southern. The depression lasted with varying intensity till the Corn Laws were repealed. A better phase of farming history was symbolized by the publication in 1840 of Liebig's *Organic Chemistry in its Application to Agriculture and Physiology* and the establishment in 1843 of the Rothamsted Experimental Station.

The Reform of the Poor Law in 1834 removed an obstruction to farming progress. It brought rate relief to the farmer in a time of difficulties and enabled him to apply labour to his farm in a more economical way. Similarly, the Repeal of the Corn Laws in 1846 defined the farmer's position in the community and forced him to rely on his own unaided efforts. Corn Laws seem to have had little influence on prices, however they may have affected the farmer's psychology. In practice, they did little more than provide jobs for officials; they were, at best, negative aids to their intended beneficiaries. When they were swept away, the farmer expected adversity. He achieved Victorian prosperity, for his potential rivals in new countries still lacked adequate transport and political quiet. But the storms were gathering: railways, steamships, refrigeration, and the cessation of foreign wars after 1870 brought successful competition and with it depression. Prices fell: the wheat acreage was contracted: the rural exodus increased in volume: wages were forced up: local government was reformed and the village labourer got the vote. From the economic aspects of this depression, English agriculture was just issuing in 1914.

The general public even began to be interested in agrarian problems. Opinion at last rebelled against reckless enclosure: it was town opinion anxious to defend the few surviving open spaces within reach of congested populations. Ironically enough, when few large areas still remained open and after some six hundred years of experience, a sound enclosure method was devised—Board of Agriculture sanction, to be gained only if the public interest were served (1893). Copyhold, the survivor of villein tenure, began rapidly to disappear, and none too soon, after 1852. Leasehold was pruned of its worst features and tenant right greatly strengthened. The village labourer, with Joseph Arch as leader and much general sympathy, took to trade unionism and won higher wages. The State embarked upon a policy of re-creating small holdings, even sanctioning the compulsory purchase of land for the purpose. Death duties and the decreasing social and economic importance of the landlord's function led to the splitting-up of the great estates. Thus experience has been reversed, and this "transfer of English land probably surpasses in extent any that has occurred since the Norman Conquest."[1]

Meanwhile, it is interesting to note that the one English village[2] where the old three-field system survives in anything like its entirety, has endured the latest of depressions with a vitality which more up-to-date neighbours might envy.

---

[1] W. H. R. Curtler, *The Enclosure and Redistribution of our Land* (1920), p. 308.

[2] Laxton in Nottinghamshire.

CHAPTER IV

THE REVOLUTION IN INDUSTRY

GREAT changes in industrial structure and method were effected in the eighteenth century. The long peace of the ministry of Walpole was a fitting prelude, and the revolution in industry began as a series of slowly determined and seemingly unconnected improvements in the technique of production. Merely to describe the successful inventions is not very helpful. Nor is it enough to explain that, necessity being the mother of invention, our Cromptons and Watts and Darbys turned their hands to the devising of new machines. "Necessity may be the mother of invention, but in her poverty she can afford very few children and birth control is a real corollary. . . . In a time of abundance of resources only can large-scale inventions and improvements be undertaken. We may then declare that Prosperity, not Necessity, is the mother of invention."[1] The industrial revolution sprang from a rich and well-prepared soil. We had built up our strength in the commercial expansion of preceding decades so surely that our economic resources now sufficed for a great industrial advance.

The inventors, moreover, rose from the same environment as Adam Smith, who investigated the Nature and Causes of the Wealth of Nations in 1776, and the younger Pitt, who in 1784 revived the Board of Trade and gave it significant economic functions. In the work of all these innovators the outlook and the ambitions of their age glowed into incandescence. If we ask why the spinning of cotton was transferred from the hand-wheel to the machine, why the steam-engine supplanted water-power, why Adam Smith attacked the authoritative regulation of economic effort, the answer is that material progress was cribbed,

[1] Sir Josiah Stamp, *On Stimulus in the Ecomonic Life* (1927), p. 63.

48

cabined and confined by methods no longer adequate to an expanding economic unity and a growing population. There were customers unsatisfied, markets only half-exploited, would-be workers only partially employed. There was an awareness of power and there were reserves of strength. The new methods, new ideas and new departures of organization came to us not merely because we needed them but because we wanted them and were well enough off to try them out and accept the changes they brought. The truth of this is established by the fact that the actual origin of particular inventions was often a matter of dispute. Why is it difficult to establish Arkwright's claim as an inventor? What were the relations of Lewis Paul to the later textile innovators? Why did Dudley's secret of the use of coal for smelting die with him and remain an enigma till Abraham Darby revived it fifty years later? Why were patents disliked in the eighteenth century? Why did the Society of Arts offer rewards to stimulate the devising of new machines? New inventions were, so to speak, in the air: the environment was favourable to industrial progress. The inventions, the improved communications, the amplifying of the financial system—all the achievements of the revolution in industry represent one movement. They were mutual determinants and all worked together for the economic good.

The revolution in industry comprised a series of improvements rather than a series of startling innovations, and these improvements were of more than one kind.[1] More than new machines and inexhaustible power of steam was required. The elaboration of large-scale manufactures necessitated the recruitment and in some cases the special training of the workers, the allocation in new ways of the workers' industrial functions, the successive conquest of processes and parts of processes by machinery, the devising of an appropiate industrial discipline for the factory as well as of the

[1] There is no better picture of the earlier phase of the revolution in industry than that given in the *Life of Robert Owen by Himself*, reprinted in 1920 (Bell).

4

factory itself, the elaboration of adequate marketing arrangements as well as the restless search for new markets. To these internal improvements which assumed, as they advanced, the character of a general development, had to be added the building up of distinct and adequate financial institutions, the reversal of the prevailing fiscal policy, and ultimately the widening of the business unit from the individual or the family firm to the joint stock company with a limitation of the investor's liability.

The history of the cotton industry has often been regarded as an epitome of the industrial revolution. It provides, of course, the outstanding example of rapid transformation, in the spinning branch at any rate. It is true, too, that "in no other modern industry can the emergence and separate organization of a wage-earning class, the development of the factory system, the story of industrial legislation and of British commercial policy in the nineteenth century be so adequately studied."[1] Yet, in more ways than one, the cotton industry differed from other industries. It was a comparatively new industry—a fresh growth grafted on to the parent stem of the woollen trade. Its youth and its comparative freedom from state regulation were conditions favourable to development which some other industries did not enjoy. Again, though the cotton industry was, like other industries in the domestic phase, organized on capitalistic lines, the new machines issued from the cottages of the manufacturers and were simple of construction, inexpensive and easily multiplied. Neither an elaborate capital outlay nor any considerable progress of engineering were necessary preliminiaries of expansion: cotton could advance by short and quick steps and the enterprising small master could keep up with and contribute towards progress. Such conditions were not true of all industries. Cotton, too, enjoyed some unique advantages. It was assisted by protectionist measures designed to help the woollen industry; and it dis-

[1] G. W. Daniels, *Early History of the Cotton Industry* (Manchester University Press, 1920). Introduction by G. Unwin, p. xxi.

covered its main source of raw material, at the very time when its expansion was assuming big proportions, outside the British Empire in a country which could no longer be controlled by our colonial system. The woollen and silk industries gained protection against printed calicoes, from India and of home produce, in 1700 and 1721, but fustians, the main branch of the Lancashire industry, were exempted from these measures: the cotton industry, that is, escaped foreign competition during its period of adolescence and achieved sufficient strength to compass the repeal of this legislation (in 1774) just when it would have become a handicap. This unforeseen result of vicarious protection helped Lancashire rather than the woollen and silk interests. The supplementing and the ultimate replacement of West Indian by American cotton was fortunate for Lancashire. Not only did it remove all difficulties about supplies of cheap raw material, for three-quarters of a century at any rate, but it enabled the cotton world to maintain a united front in the attack on the whole system of trade regulation.

The cotton industry was thus well placed for rapid growth. Its raw material was cheap and expansion of supplies presented no insuperable difficulties. Its finished product was inexpensive and light; growing markets were therefore easy of discovery. The fibre was standardized by nature and lent itself readily to manipulation by machinery. In Lancashire particularly the climate was well suited to cotton manufacture, though the importance of humidity was not fundamental until the manufacture of fine cottons was undertaken. The industry had early attracted substantial merchants, so that capital and organization were not lacking. A specialized body of industrious and inventive workers, with a habit of combination, had already by the middle of the century differentiated themselves from the farmer-manufacturers or part-time industrialists who were still available, however, as auxiliaries. In an industry so circumstanced, inventions came with comparative ease. A few decades of effort and achievement sufficed for the complete transformation of the spinning industry, for the beginning of new methods of bleaching (1786) and calico-printing (1784), for the establishment of the factory organization, and for an intense localization of all branches of the cotton manufacture in Lancashire.

A few leading points may be stressed in the history thus summarized. The great difficulty of the cotton industry in mid-century was the slowness of spinning. This branch, in which, too, technical problems were simpler, was the first to be mechanized. The Hargreaves jenny (about 1767: patented 1770) had at first eight, and within twenty years eighty spindles. The Arkwright water-frame (patents 1769 and 1775) produced stronger yarn and was from the outset a power-machine. Crompton's mule (1779) made possible the machine-manufacture of fine cottons, but it required improvement and enlargement before it became suitable for power-spinning. These had been effected by 1790, by which time the problem of yarn supplies was solved and a new organization shaped. The steam-engine then began to be adopted as the ordinary source of power, and cheaper grades of labour, women and children that is, were recruited. Whitney's cotton-gin (1794) made American cotton cleaner and more abundant than any other, and in strengthening the hold of the system of slavery, kept it cheap. The cotton industry then ceased to be a poor relation of the woollen manufacture: it became our leading export industry, and the routes of the world's trade in cotton cloths radiated outwards from Manchester.

There are certain points of similarity in the history of the potteries. "The revolution in the potteries consisted in the discovery by constant experiment of new bodies, new glazes, new methods of decoration; a greater division of labour, a growth of the factory and the development of methods of control, i.e., the beginnings of scientific management and cost accounting; the improvement of transportation and the opening of new markets at home and abroad."[1]

[1] V. W. Bladen, "The Potteries in the Industrial Revolution", in *Economic Journal* (Economic History Supplement), Jan. 1926.

In the expansion of the potteries, the influence of individual leadership (Wedgwood's) and of transport improvements, more particularly of canals, counted for more than in the case of the cotton industry, but the general factors of expansion were similar. Yet the effect on the labouring population was different. Pottery remained a skilled worker's trade. It had its burden of evils—the potters won no "charter of health" till 1891—but among these the destruction of craftsmanship by machinery was not included.

The other textiles provide a contrast with cotton. Wool lagged far behind. It was hampered by ancient legislation imposing awkward standards of size and quality, and by a network of protective duties; it was held up still more by the scarcity of raw material, supplies of which were not greatly enlarged till the Australian clip became available in the 1830s. Power-driven machinery came only slowly, therefore—first in spinning and carding, then in weaving, and lastly in combing. In 1847 a traveller observed near Leeds "whole fields of teazles in flower . . . which no effort of the mechanician has as yet enabled him to supersede" for the work of raising the nap of the finer broadcloths. The woollen manufacture had not yet attained conditions which made expansion irresistible. Like the weaving branch in cotton, it awaited the convergence of open markets, technical progress and strong incentives to develop the economy of large factories. Similarly, the linen industry, with new machinery available in the 1790s, the hosiery trade, endowed with a singularly precocious machine in Elizabeth's reign, the silk manufacture, which achieved machinery and factories before cotton, all had some of the factors of rapid expansion. Of the textiles, cotton had an environment, general and particular, favourable to rapid expansion in the period between 1750 and 1850.

The iron industry offers an interesting comparison with that of cotton, for while the latter was progressive from its inception, the former was moribund in the early eighteenth century. Charcoal was its fuel and a timber-famine prevailed in the older centres of manufacture. Iron-making plant was becoming semi-nomadic, moving even to remote places in search of charcoal yet obviously dependent on water-communications. An alternative fuel to charcoal was the first condition of escape from this unhealthy situation.

Coke was the new fuel. Though successfully employed in Darby's works at Coalbrookdale from about 1709 and accompanied by the introduction of better methods of casting iron, the new technique had not become the general practice till half a century had elapsed. Yet it brought a wide extension of the use of cast-iron and for a time overshadowed the hitherto more important wrought-iron branch of the industry. Progress in wrought-iron was an urgent need and was the aim of many experimenters. When Cort patented the grooved roller (1783) and the puddling process (1784), success was achieved. The steam-engine gave the necessary power, and the iron industry was at last able to escape from its slough of despond and to supply the world with the capital goods, the materials of construction and the varied articles of popular use which were so urgently needed. The industrial significance of what had been accomplished was illustrated when the Carron works was founded in 1759. From the outset Carron was conceived on a big scale: it adopted the latest practice: it initiated an industrial revolution in Scotland: it gave Watt his entrance into industry. It foreshadowed the great industry of our own day.

The history of the steam-engine gives a pretty complete picture of the revolution in industry. Neither in spirit nor in fact is the legend of Watt and the kettle true. Much experience in the industrial use of steam-power preceded Watt's invention. Though the usual source of power was still the water-wheel, the Newcomen engine (1706) had been useful as a means of pumping water from mines and as a means of providing an artificial fall of water for power purposes. But neither the Newcomen engine nor the first Watt engine (1769) was more than a steam pump. Watt's engine was preferable because its fuel costs were low.

Where that was not a major consideration, it made little appeal. The patent for rotary motion (1781) grew out of the earlier work of Watt, but it took a good many years before it was commonly realized that Watt had solved thereby the world's power-problems. Progress, that is, was not automatic in this or other industries, and it sprang from the collaboration of circumstances and individuals alike. Matthew Boulton, in partnership with whom Watt perfected his engine, was a model of progressiveness of outlook, method and organization. His Birmingham factory was large, well-run and full of ingenious machinery; it was staffed by skilled workers whom Boulton had had to train; it offered Watt useful collaborators as well as a congenial and favourable environment. Had Crompton met similar co-operation and encouragement, the advance of cotton would have been even more rapid than it was. Boulton's command of capital, his imagination and patience, his knowledge, based on experience, of business needs all counted in the evolution of the steam-engine. The steam-engine, too, would have penetrated industry even more slowly than it did save that it offered generous economies in the use of fuel. Its power possibilities were only slowly grasped. When they were, the advent of large-scale manufacture and its localization near coal supplies came quite inevitably; coal and iron were then finally yoked together as the material basis of our industrial civilization. Thus the steam-engine, like the other inventions, only attained universality when the environment was favourable. Watt was a great inventor, but he was the child of his age. His steam-engine was a magnificent achievement, but it was not a mere personal triumph.

No group of trades shows more clearly than engineering the character of the industrial transition. William Fairbairn, a mason's labourer who became a great captain of industry and President of the British Association, composed a Treatise on Mills and Millwork (1863). "The millwright of former days," he wrote, "was to a great extent the sole representative of mechanical art . . . the engineer of the district in which he lived, a kind of jack-of-all-trades, who could with equal facility work at the lathe, the anvil or the carpenter's bench." The history of the engineering industry is largely the history of the splitting up of the millwright's numerous functions. The steam-engine and the demands of the new machine industries were the chief agencies in this process. Manufacturers increasingly called upon the engineers for specialized products. The ingenuity of Maudslay and Bramah in the devising of machine tools enabled these demands to be met: the steam-engine having solved the problem of power, big firms soon began to supplant the small pioneers of engineering. The result was that "whenever capital comes forward to take advantage of an improved demand for goods, the means of fructifying it are provided with such rapidity, that it may realize its own amount in profit, ere an analogous factory could be set a-going in France, Belgium or Germany."[1]

Civil engineering, too, began to be differentiated from mechanical engineering, so great was the call for bridges, harbour-works, canals, and the other agencies of improved transport. In the Charter of Incorporation (1828) of the Institute of Civil Engineers, "the profession" of a civil engineer was defined as that of "the art of directing the Great Sources of Power in Nature for the use and convenience of man." Yet the detailed description of what was included in that art omitted collieries, steam-engines, metallurgy, gas and railways. Already considerable advance in these branches of specialized engineering had been made. Engineering clearly was taking big strides. In all its branches it was directed particularly to the needs of the towns and the industries located in them, and ministering to them. The rise of engineering was the mark of an urban civilization. It brought too a great widening of the avenues of employment open to the skilled worker. The constructive aspects of the revolution in industry are in no group of trades more clearly exemplified.

[1] A. Ure, *Philosophy of Manufacture* (1835), p. 39.

CHAPTER V

The Revolution in Communications

"THE expense of making and maintaining the public roads in any country," wrote Adam Smith, "must evidently increase with the annual produce of the land and labour of that country, or with the quantity and weight of the goods which it becomes necessary to fetch and carry upon these roads." The actual road-problem in the eighteenth century was greater than increasing use and costs: it was these complicated by lack of engineering skill, by unwise legislation, and by the defects of local government. River improvement, on which large sums were spent in the first half of the century, had made an important contribution to economic progress, but as the century wore on it became increasingly clear that more was being asked of our means of internal communication than they were designed to bear. Road deterioration became evident, and river transport stayed costly. The economic unification of the country was retarded and the growth of business handicapped.

The need for better means of communication was apparent to politician, landowner and man of business alike. The Jacobite rebellion of 1745 had demonstrated the danger of leaving remote areas in their age-long isolation. Political reasons combined with economic to assure Parliamentary encouragement to road construction. Turnpike trusts, therefore, were established, each with a specified responsibility. Local government being a name rather than a reality, and compulsory labour being inadequate, no other means than the toll-charging turnpike presented itself. The trusts were never popular, their toll-bars were quite frequently attacked with violence, but they were found to be indispensable. Their original lease of twenty-one years of life was extended and a large number of the trusts did their work conscientiously if at a high cost to the users.

But the road difficulties were greater than the trusts could surmount. There were bad patches even on the main routes—neglected links which deserved all the abuse heaped upon them by Arthur Young and other travellers. Some trusts were inefficient. Local roads were left to the parishes with unpaid officers and only compulsory and pauper labour at their command. Bridges were the affair of the county. There was no adequate technique of road construction. There was a bewildering variety of unrepealed laws regulating the structure of vehicles and the weight of loads. It was not, in fact, till the dawning of the railway age that the road system was rendered completely satisfactory. By that time the blind Metcalfe had shown how roads could be built on boggy ground; Telford how new roads should be engineered; Macadam how old roads could be made as good as new. Smeaton, Rennie and Telford built bridges as well as docks, canals and lighthouses, and the iron industry had contributed the iron bridge.

Contemporaneous with the road improvements of George III's reign was the elaboration of a canal system. The canal was not a new thing even in England, for Vermuyden had been brought over with Dutch labour from Holland under the Commonwealth to drain the water-logged Fen country. But the Duke of Bridgewater initiated in 1759 what was for this country a new use for artificial waterways when he employed Brindley to build a canal between his coal pits at Worsley and their market in Manchester (1759–61). The economic success of this enterprise led to a rapid multiplication of canals. These early canals were a great success. They contributed with an astonishing vigour to the economic growth of the districts they served. Old towns were invigorated; new ones were established. The mobility of raw materials and manufactured goods was increased and cheapened. The prices of goods of all sorts were reduced. and the bad-weather isolation of many places hitherto dependent on roads was ended. Even an alternative mode of personal travel was made available. It would be difficult, in fact, to exaggerate the value of the new canals, and one is left wondering why they had not been built earlier. For this, doubtless, there were many reasons. Most parts of the country were near the sea. The rise of heavy industries was late in coming. In any case, an intrepid initiator with adequate resources was required to show the way: even the Duke of Bridgewater was in straits more than once in meeting his enormous obligations. It was only with the growth of the cotton industry, too, that men's minds were turned to the problems and possibilities of artificial waterways. River improvement did not lead to canal building, as might have been expected, till in 1755 a scheme was sanctioned for the improvement of the Sankey Brook on the Mersey by means of a "cut" $11\frac{1}{2}$ miles long. The reluctance of landlords, who feared damage to their estates and lacked the imagination to see that an increase of values would follow, was pretty general. But, like merchants and manufacturers they came to see that there was money to be made out of canals and took shares in them. The result was a canal boom in the early nineties which led to the promotion of schemes that were economically and financially unwise.

In their best days, after Waterloo, the canals were not rich investments. Very few of them showed high profits, such as the 40 per cent. of the Mersey and Irwell. The reverse rather was the case. "It is a well-known fact," wrote McCulloch,[1] "that canals, at an average, and allowing for the length of time that must elapse from the first outlay of capital before they yield any return, are not very productive. . . . On the whole they seem to have been more beneficial to the public than to their projectors." Perhaps it was unfortunate, both for canals and later for railways, that the canal companies were not carriers. They were regarded as alternatives to the highway and it was not till 1845 that they

[1] McCullock, *Dictionary of Commerce.* Article on canals.

were authorized to do transport business. It was then too late for comprehensive improvements to be made. Their original defects of construction and size became more and more obvious. In many cases the railway companies acquired the central links of a large number of them with the intention of rendering them ineffective competitors, but this they were often forced to do by the canal companies themselves, which barred their way to and from important points. The modernizing of the canal system has been discussed more than once since a "creeping paralysis" (as the 1883 Committee termed it) descended upon them after 1840. But it has never been worth anybody's while to do it.

RAILWAYS

Railways require a special track and a special locomotive, and both were worked out in connection with colleries. Many had experimented with road locomotives in the eighteenth as well as the nineteenth century. But nothing came of these efforts. It was George Stephenson who, after some years of experience as engine-wright of a Northumberland colliery, set up a locomotive in 1814 which drew coal over the six miles between the colliery and the Tyne. In the next few years he improved his engine, set up a locomotive and rail factory, and began to plan railways. Thus the two lines of development were united, and the railway as we know it became a possibility. The Stockton–Darlington (1825) and the Manchester–Liverpool (1830) Railways were persuaded to adopt the locomotive engine. The former revealed the first principles of operation, the disadvantages of the common user system, and the value of the railway for handling goods: the latter proved beyond doubt the superiority in speed and convenience of the railway for carrying passengers as well as goods. After 1830 the railway began its career of world conquest.

The English railways were built piecemeal. Uncertainties about the locomotive and the advocacy of the stationary engine, atmospheric engine, and its other rivals were dissipated by 1840. In the late thirties the main lines out of London were built, and a phase of local construction in different parts of the country culminated in the railway boom of 1845–7, by which time some 200 railway companies had been established and 5,127 miles opened for traffic (1848). The consolidation of local lines followed, and the building up of through communications. The Great Western did not abandon its broad 7-foot gauge till 1892 for the narrower gauge of 4 feet 8½ inches which Stephenson had adopted and which Parliament in 1846 declared to be the British standard. The Railway Clearing House was established in 1842 to balance up the payments for through traffic over different lines. The railways made agreements among themselves about matters of common concern. Thus the growing-pains were gradually eased and a technique of operation was developed.

To summarize the services rendered by railways to the community is a large task. It is easy to ante-date their period of great significance: there were, after all, only 9,000 miles of railway opened for use in 1854. But even in the first half of the century they did big things. They brought a mitigation of the long distress of the post-Waterloo period by opening up new avenues of permanent employment: it was not the revision of the Poor Law but the expanding employment directly on work of construction and then of operation, and indirectly on the various trades which contributed to railway initiation and maintenance, which enabled the workers to leave behind the hunger of the thirties and forties. Improved communications stimulated the industrial and commercial expansion of the new manufacturing areas and confirmed the localization already effected. The new network of communications widely extended personal mobility and facilitated further urbanization. The railways broke the monopoly of the canal companies, as the canals had of the river navigation companies—cheaper transport meant cheaper prices, with an attendant train of advantages to all classes. They brought elements of certainty into business, because railways could run to time, and quicker handling of goods enabled merchants to keep shorter stocks and to work on shorter, and therefore less expensive, credits. They encouraged new habits of investment among new classes of investors, and the Stock Exchange achieved a wide significance in consequence. They forced the State to face questions of monopoly, and of the regulation of monopoly, in the very hey-day of individualism. Indirectly, they did more than any other simple agency to break the prestige of the landed aristocracy, and they assured the continuance of the expansion of industries into the future. The influence of railways is best summed up, perhaps, in the statement that Great Britain became an economic unity.

To their internal effects must be added the result of the careers of such contractors as Brassey. That addition is in large measure the story of the export of capital, of the new imperialism and of the intensified rivalries which culminated in the debacle of 1914–18.

SHIPPING

The progress of shipping was conditioned by the pressure of war and of fiscal policy. War brought a heavy toll of shipping losses: the Navigation Acts protected the British shipowner from foreign competition: the timber duties made the material of construction expensive. The growing volume of trade necessitated a great expansion of the mercantile marine in the eighteenth century, but improvement in the construction of the sailing ship came from the United Sates rather than this country. The wars in which this country was engaged gave the Americans a great chance, and they took it. The American clipper was the fastest vessel afloat till the British shipbuilders copied it. New construction on up-to-date lines then combined with the building of important harbour works to produce great developments, alike in old ports like London and Bristol and in new ones like Liverpool and Glasgow.

In ocean shipping the wooden sailing-vessel more than held its own until the sixties of the nineteenth century. Even in the eighteenth century, however, bold experiments in the use of iron for construction and of the steam-engine for motive power were made in this country and in the United States. Considerable success in steamer construction had been achieved by 1830 but it was limited to inland waters and narrow seas. The early steam-using boats on the open seas relied on sails with steam-driven paddles as auxiliaries, a system which lasted till well after 1850. The Post Office, after a limited and not very successful experience of State-owned vessels, offered subsidies for mail services which brought into being the Cunard, the Peninsular and Oriental and the Royal Mail Steam Packet Companies between 1837 and 1840. But progress was not very rapid till the invention of the compound engine (1854), the establishment of coaling-stations, and the building of large vessels with iron hulls. The liner services then developed rapidly, and ocean-going tramps were able to pioneer new services and to gather occasional cargoes as well as the great seasonal cargoes of foodstuffs and raw materials.

There were ups and downs in this record of gradual progress. After 1815 the British mercantile marine had to face a prolonged depression when freights fell and tonnage was superfluous. In this period English shipping did not always carry too good a name. More than one inquiry was made into the causes of the distressing frequency of wrecks. Inefficient construction was encouraged by the faulty system of classification employed by Lloyd's—rectified in 1839—and the appointment of untrained masters and officers was all too common. There were some eight hundred vessels wrecked in 1833, of which, according to insurance brokers, nearly half might be ascribed to the ignorance, incapacity and carelessness of the masters and crews.[1]

[1] McCulloch, *Dictionary of Commerce*, Supplement to 1835 edition, p. 41.

Drunkenness was habitual on board; the conditions of ship-life in general were in many ways comparable with those prevalent in the worst factories. Such Acts as that of 1835, which established a Seamen's Register, did something to stimulate improvement, but it looked back as much as forward. We had to wait till 1876 for the Plimsoll Line.

To these agencies of communication by land and sea must be added the modern post office, the telegraph, the cable, and the newspaper.

CHAPTER VI

WARS AND POPULATION

IN the hundred years between 1750 and 1850, the pressure of wars was extremely heavy. Before recovery from the Seven Years' War (1756–63) and the War of American Independence (1774–84) was yet complete, the conflagrations (1793–1815) which sprang from the French Revolution flamed out. From these agonies an exhausted Europe required some thirty years of convalescence. The great economic and social transformation was effected, that is, in a century of stress.

All wars necessitate the withdrawal of man-power for combatant purposes. They involve expenditure upon war material—an expenditure which is economically wasteful—and, capital and energy being diverted to the making of it, wars distort the normal direction of industry and trade. They are all too commonly financed by expedients which would not be tolerated in peace-time; and they disturb existing tendencies in the distribution of the nation's income. They evoke or accentuate reactionary habits of thought and so produce policies or repressions characteristic of the war mind. They leave their aftermath of debt, impoverishment and trade depression, and the war mind is often maintained in the peace years, filling them with a disillusion from which also recovery has to be made. None of these consequences of war is trifling, and in sum they represent a great burden. The coincidence of such factors with the great industrial developments, is of first-rate importance.

"It is not unreasonable to suggest," writes Professor Daniels, "that if peace had prevailed instead of war, trade and employment would have been steadier; that prices, especially food prices, would have been more stable; that

5

social conditions would have received more adequate attention; and that workpeople would have been in a better position to protect their economic interests. . . . When the conditions that prevailed in the first part of the nineteenth century are regarded in the light of these considerations, it is difficult to resist the conclusion that the war, and not the industrial revolution, was the dominant factor in their determination."[1] Such an interpretation is attractive and likely to appeal to a generation whose lives are conditioned by the same relentless pressure. It does obviously contain a great deal of truth. But there are some things which it does not explain. A considerable factor in the social distress of the period was the immigration of Irish labourers with their potato standards, their willingness to live in any sort of hovel, and their ready acceptance of extremely low wages. The familiar use of the term "paddy" to describe a builder's labourer suggests that they well-nigh monopolized certain grades of unskilled work. The nastiest quarters in northern industrial towns were usually those where the Irish were herded together. The wars were not the cause of this immigration. Nor could the degradation which characterized the mining centres be ascribed to the wars. Conditions of serfdom prevailed in Scottish mines down to 1799, and of something regrettably similar in some mining areas in England. That disgusting conditions in the mines did not shock England till 1842 was not due to war pressure. The exploitation of women and children and pauper apprentices was not occasioned by the war, nor was the antipathy to workers' combinations, which for generations had fallen under the law of conspiracy and under particular Acts of Parliament. The dominant factor in determining the condition of the first half of the nineteenth century was rather that those conditions were inherited, hence a conscience about them, even an awareness of them, grew only slowly. The war's share in them was that exhaustion, disillusion and

[1] G. W. Daniels. "The Industrial Revolution in the Light of Recent Research" in *Journal of Adult Education*, April 1928.

distrust delayed both their recognition and their remedying: it intensified the bad, even caused retrogression, but not more. The new industrialists were the opponents of, for instance, factory legislation. They strove for freedom to control their enterprises as they willed. But that attitude was not born of war, and was inimical to the development of an ideal of social justice.

It would be a mistake, all the same, to understate the consequences of the wars. Had they not exerted so prolonged an influence towards social and economic impoverishment, the great legislative triumphs of post-Waterloo England would have been something better than the reformed Poor Law and the meagre measure of parliamentary reform of 1832. Had there been no wars, the expansion of foreign trade would have steadily progressed: as it was, foreign trade advanced but little in 1850. The nation's poverty of mind and estate was conditioned by the lack of markets, home and foreign. That lack slowed up the industrial expansion. It is a common view that the industrial changes were sweeping and cataclysmic: save in the case of cotton-spinning, the rapid progress of which brought a brief prosperity to spinners, the industrial changes came too slowly. They came so slowly that the bad was always being preserved: a speedier onset would have swept it away, because its inefficiency would have been revealed.

It is difficult to make any positive statement about the effect of the wars on the growth of population. The direct losses of man-power in the wars of the eighteenth century were kept down by the use of subsidies, sea-power and hired Continental mercenaries, and were not nearly so heavy as those of the French wars. In these heavy recruitments had to be made. A careful contemporary maintained that the proportion of men in arms during the French wars was larger in this country than in any other state in Europe. Yet the rate of growth, so far as defective figures allow of a judgment, does not seem to have suffered greatly.

In the eighteenth century few people were interested in the

facts or problems of population. Politicians did not regard such matters as important: why should they? They had very few constituents to consider and in any case votes could be bought. There were no social services save the Poor Law, and when recruits were required for army or navy, there was no difficulty in just taking those that were required. A few people dabbled in "political arithmetic" or were interested in the growth of insurance: to them national or individual resources were matters of importance about which exact knowledge would have value. But in general there was indifference, even hostility, to the idea of an enumeration of the population. Hence in 1753 when it was proposed to take a census, the plan was defeated. "I did not believe," said the Member for York, "that there had been any individual of the human species, so presumptuous and so abandoned, as to make the proposal." To satisfy the curiosity of the political arithmeticians would destroy "the last remains of English liberty"; it would give foreign foes a knowledge of our weakness, and foes at home a knowledge of our strength; it would lead to new taxation; it would cost £50,000; besides it could not be done because so many people were unable to write. The House of Lords could be relied upon to deal faithfully with any measure which might induce increased taxation, and so no census was taken till 1801. By then things had changed. The problem of poverty, or of the Poor Law, had become oppressive. The bogey of over-population had been raised. A possible method had been shown to be practicable in 1786 when an inquiry was made into poor rates. The pressure of war had brought a new attitude. Hence from 1801 onwards at ten-year intervals a census has been taken and useful knowledge has been made available. The early enumerations provide a basis upon which quite reasonably accurate calculations can rest. The Census of 1871 retraced the ground and arrived at the following figures of the total population of England and Wales estimated to mid-year in each case:

1801   9,192,810

1811	...	...	10,467,728
1821	...	...	12,190,175
1831	...	...	14,070,681
1841	...	...	16,049,554
1851	...	...	18,109,410

To these figures must be added estimates for the eighteenth century, if the general movement of numbers is to be appreciated. Here the ground is both difficult and technical, but has been made the subject of very close study in recent years.[1] The importance of this work is that on it depends to some considerable extent the social interpretation of the economic changes of our period. It is not merely that the environment of Malthus is under consideration: if it is possible to discover the broad tendencies, the quality of the civilization of the epoch gets some illumination. For these tendencies depend on birth-rates, death-rates and marriage-rates, and they are, presumably, largely determined by social conditions. At the beginning of the eighteenth century the population of England and Wales approximated to 5,800,000. It was about 6,250,000 in 1750, and had increased by 1780 to 7,500,000.

It is clear, then, that the period of the Industrial Revolution showed a steady increase in numbers. The Malthusian view was that this rate of increase was too rapid, being unhealthily swollen by economic factors of a preventable kind. Until lately, it has been commonly held that this increase was due to high birth-rates, and in spite of high death-rates, and that these high birth-rates were due to the poor law and to the prevalence of child labour, which appealed to the cupidity of some parents and to the needs of still more. But this interpretation is not tenable without qualification. The birth-rate had an upwards tendency from

[1] See G. T. Griffith, *Population Problems of the Age of Malthus* (1926), M. C. Buer, *Health, Wealth and Population in the Early Days of the Industrial Revolution* (1926), and a valuable article by T. H. Marshall on "The Population Problem during the Industrial Revolution" in the *Economic Journal* (Economic History Supplement), January 1929.

1710 to 1810. It showed a slight fall from then to 1840, when a sharp drop set in. But prior to 1840, at any rate, there is no startling movement of the birth-rate, and the remarkable increase of population cannot be adequately explained in that way. In the case of the death-rate, a very remarkable movement did take place. It fell in a degree that had no precedent. The death-rate had always been high, and was at its highest—higher, for example, than the birth-rate in 1730 —in the years when excessive gin-drinking was a popular habit. The worst years of this mania, though not of other forms of excessive alcoholism, were over by the middle of the century. From about 1750 the death-rate steadily declined, the fall being sharp from 1780 onwards. In the years following 1815 this decline was arrested, but there was no return to the very high figures of the earlier eighteenth century. It was this fall in the death-rate which was the dominating factor in the increase of population.

To what was this lessening death-rate due? It coincided with an expansion of economic power, and was so definite that even the war-losses elude estimation. Just how and how far it was linked with contemporaneous material progress is not easily determined. "Perhaps the most impressive thing which has come out of the statistical study of human population is the evidence that the steady onward march of this growth is not sensibly influenced by the host of economic and social events which are supposed by logical necessity to affect it."[1] Failing ultimate explanations, we have to be content to associate the falling death-rate with the progress of medical science and public health measures. In these directions the eighteenth century was a progressive period. London set the example of better housing, drainage, paving and water-supply. Hospitals and dispensaries were built, and better medical services provided in them. Other towns followed this example and so the mortality springing from epidemic diseases was reduced. The infantile death-

[1] R. Pearl, *Proceedings of the World Population Conference*, 1927, p. 30.

rate was reduced also, and the practices of inoculation (1722) and vaccination (1798) were introduced and extended.

The progress of the eighteenth century was definite and considerable. But unfortunately "there was a natural ebb in the tide of public health reform. . . . Medical science tended to fall into a rut after a period of achievement. . . . The best minds in the medical profession, like those in other spheres, were much occupied with administrative abuses and with the building up of a reasonable professional organization."[1] Hence, at the very time when urban concentrations were taking shape most rapidly, the "natural ebb" set in with its disheartening effects. The great effort, inspired by Chadwick, to create a national public health service was defeated at a period of most urgent need, defeated by the defects of local government as well as the preoccupations of the medical profession, by ignorance and prejudice in high places and low, as well as by the active hostility of vested interests concerned to maintain their profits (e.g. out of water-supply) at whatever social cost.

It has been suggested that the dominant factor in the expansion of numbers was the fall in the death-rate. The birth-rate, however, cannot be ignored. While it shows no movement so striking as the downward leap of the death-rate after 1780, it was still very high when compared with the rates of preceding and later periods. The decline in infant-mortality was such that this maintenance of a high birth-rate is surprising. It seems likely that the explanation of it is to be found, after all, in the Poor Law and the prevalence of child labour. Economic adversity did, it would seem, have an effect such as Malthus deplored. If so, sentimentalism and industrial capitalism exacted a pretty heavy toll. The working-classes waxed fruitful and multiplied not because they believed that in the multitude of the people was the Kingdom's glory, but because they needed the pittances of the Poor Law and of their children's premature labour.

[1] M. C. Buer, *Health, Wealth and Population*, pp. 233-4.

CHAPTER VII

THE NEW INDUSTRIALISM

THE true character of the new industrialism is not easily described. Was the England which issued from the industrial revolution the England of Charles Dickens or of the classical economists (caricatured as "dismal") or of Cobdenite Manchester or of the Society for the Diffusion of Useful Knowledge or of the Chartists? Was it the "two Englands" of Disraeli or the tyranny painted by the anti-Capitalists or the ill-shapen futility seen by Carlyle? The historian has to rely on the voices which were articulate in his period, and they all sang different songs. To some people in these (and any) decades England was obviously going to the dogs—the well-off and the badly-off may be expected at any time to agree on this. To others, especially to those who were able to force their way up the new avenues to wealth, the opposite was true. Whatever the tones of the picture presented as a portrait of the new industrialism, they will be composed from the varying colours of contemporary view, intermingled with the knowledge gained from subsequent experience.

Seen from a distance, the expanding industries went from strength to strength: looked at closely, there were ups and downs. Different industries were given over to a new manufacturing technique at varying rates, cotton-spinning rapidly, for instance, but weaving slowly. Some, like coal, were enlarged without achieving much in the way of a new technique. Some started, like shipbuilding, from a highly capitalistic basis: others, like Sheffield cutlery, were still, and long remained, in the hands of small and mechanically not progressive masters. In an old capitalistic industry like coal-mining, conditions of employment for men, women and

72

children were unvaryingly bad throughout the period of the industrial revolution: in a new industry like cotton, the first impact of the new methods was beneficial to the workers and only with the rise of the steam-factories, which coincided with the onset of the French wars, did conditions become distressful. Again, manufacturers were constantly brought up against changes in the conditions of competition. The general economic environment was disturbed by war conditions, and the particular economic environment of each industry and each locality by the successes and failures of experiments in organization and with new machines. In sum the progress made was a progress by fits and starts. "The capitalists, the owners of factories and heads of manufacturing and commercial undertakings, moved forward like a disorderly mob to the conquest of markets."[1] Thus the increased power of production often got ahead of the power of consumption, and unemployment of capital and labour followed till the balance was rectified and a new start became possible.

The new manufacturing technique aimed at the removal of impediments to increased production. Allowance having been made for failures as well as successes and for the step-by-step character of the advance, it is a safe general statement that increased production was achieved. This obvious feature of the new industrialism is worth stressing because ultimately in some measure everyone stood to gain. The increased manufacture of cotton goods necessitated an enlarged demand for the raw material, from about 8,000 tons in 1760 to over 300,000 tons (excluding re-exported cotton) in 1850. The make of iron increased from about 20,000 tons to over 2,000,000 tons in the same period. The British output of coal was under 5,000,000 tons in 1750, and a century later was twelve times as great. Examples need not be multiplied. Along with these increases there came a cheapening of commodities, and an equally marked increase in the volume of employment. The Society for the Diffusion

[1] E. Halévy, *History of the English People in 1815*, p. 271.

of Useful Knowledge tried to reconcile the working-man to machinery by issuing at one shilling a small volume entitled *The Results of Machinery, namely Cheap Production and Increased Employment Exhibited.* The book was beyond most working-men's pockets and erudition, but it gave irrefutable facts and arguments upon questions on which they agreed with the authors. "The spinning machinery in Lancashire alone," it declared, "produced, in 1825, as much yarn as would have required twenty-one million three hundred and twenty thousand persons to produce with the distaff and spindle." It admitted that "there are degrees in the agreeable nature of the employment" but pointed out that cotton cloths which used to cost six shillings a yard were being sold for sixpence. It is absurd to regard the industrial revolution as compounded of evils: if it were so, they had a useful soul of goodness. The old methods of production, in fact, were quite inadequate to the support of a growing population. The positive checks to population, according to Malthus, included "all unwholesome occupations, severe labour and exposure to the seasons, extreme poverty, bad nursing of children, great towns, excesses of all kinds, the whole train of common diseases and epidemics, war, plague and famine." This list of horrors seemed, unhappily, to be a description of the consequence of the new industrialism to very many workers in factory, field and mine, and so the ultimately beneficent effects of the new system of manufacture were concealed. But the broad view over a long period shows unmistakably improved standards of life for a larger population. It was a pity that so large a proportion of the workers could not measure their lives in long periods.

Unfortunately it is not possible to stop at that point. The fact that the industrial revolution proceeded slowly, unevenly and not always placidly, is equally unmistakable. To paint it as a period of unrelieved gloom is as untrue as to stress only its contributions to material progress. The coming of machinery meant, sooner or later, the coming of factories. It has often been pointed out that there were factories before the eighteenth century. The Weavers Act of 1555, and the half-legendary achievements of Jack of Newbury and other heroes of Deloney's Tales show in the woollen industry the engrossing of looms by employers and their collection in large industrial units. But the economies of such experiments were negative rather than positive. They would eliminate such characteristic evils of the domestic system as the embezzlement of raw material and would keep the quality of workmanship under constant supervision, but they did not make possible any major economy. The time came, too, when improvements would be lost sight of if the factory did not, as it were, keep them together. One of the great figures of the cotton industry in its early days of expansion made the significant remark that, before the coming of the great inventions, the endeavour to find better methods "filled cottages with little improvements", and this multiplication of instruments was forcing the work out of cottages. "Here," he declared, "commences the factory system."[1] We may agree, then, that it was not the factory which was new but the conditions which made it a necessary form of industrial organization. The factory was the symbol and the agency of industrial capitalism. Capitalism itself was no new thing. Systems of slavery and serfdom were obviously capitalistic, and in a true sense the machine is the latter-day substitute for the slave. But before the industrial revolution, the commercial capitalist was the centre of the economic system, organizing production and therefore employment. With the coming of the factory, the industrial specialist rose not merely to prominence but to leadership. The landed proprietor, entrenched in ancient privilege and with a dominating grasp of the political machine, the great merchants and merchant bankers profitably enjoying very close financial relationships with their governments and accumulating wealth from their handling

[1] Kennedy, in *Transactions of the Manchester Literary and Philosophical Society*, Vol. III, pp. 118-9.

of wholesale trade, moved in a different economic and social environment from that of the manufacturer, a word which may describe master or artisan. But with the coming of the factory this was changed. In the "Gehenna of manufacturing Radicalism," as Carlyle called the North of England, and a little later in the Birmingham and Sheffield areas and in the woollen towns of Yorkshire, the "captain of industry" rose to unmistakable significance. When, as was the case with Sir Robert Peel's father, he could leave a fortune of a million and a half, accumulated out of cotton, he was clearly a person of account. It would be hazardous to call him an average manufacturer, though there were many successful industrialists who, like him, made their own way from rural insignificance, directly or at one or two removes. Failures, too, were probably commoner than successes in this climbing process. The comparatively slow development of big-scale manufacture, and its passage through the less expensive water-power phase before the final phase of steam-power and elaborate iron machinery, enabled the bolder pioneers to keep pace with the improving technique. But the stage soon came when command of wide resources was essential to manufacturing success: with it had to be combined, or procured, skill in the management of masses of men, women and children, and in the allocation of their labour, and efficient knowledge of actual and possible markets. Such people soon learned how to safeguard their interests: they formed under Wedgwood's leadership a General Chamber of Manufacturers, for instance, to attack in 1785 Pitt's commercial treaty between England and Ireland; in 1782 a group of cotton manufacturers had secured from Parliament sharp legislation against loom-breaking, and in 1799 an employers' "black book" of difficult workmen is complained of in Bolton. It might take a long time before they achieved a political and social prestige commensurate with their economic position—a delay due partly at least to the Nonconformist persuasion of so many of them—but their economic power could not be questioned.

It was they who entered upon the anti-Corn Law struggle, which was a direct attack upon the landed interest; they were the true parents of the railway system, which, without their initiative and backing, might have remained for long concealed in the special service of the mines; they were the makers of the new industrial towns, built like their mills with due regard to their own immediate interests but with a haste, an ignorance, and a disregard for the elementary amenities of life for which later generations have ever since been paying heavily. Civilization has been defined as "the use to which an age puts its resources of wealth, knowledge and power, in order to create a social life." These self-confident, acquisitive, and in their narrow sphere, efficient captains of industry were the architects of our civilization. Their ideals can be read quite plainly in the railways, the bridges, the harbours, the delicate machinery and the other material triumphs of the Victorian era: these things are to this later age what the very different achievements of the Renaissance were to the fifteenth century. Their limitations, equally, are apparent in the back-to-back houses, the wage-cutting habits, the transportation of Dorchester labourers, the coffin-ships against which Plimsoll struggled almost alone.

Industrial capitalism was the embodiment of a gospel of competition. That gospel explains much of the success and many of the weaknesses of the new masters of civilization. It has, of course, a long historical ancestry, and premonitions of its ultimate victory may be found in the Puritan revolution. But it attained maturity during the industrial revolution, and acquired the authority of a religious belief, of a belief which did in fact govern conduct. The factory achieved its unsavoury reputation partly because its creators believed in their right to do what they would, short of detection in breaking the law, with their own, and "their own" seemed to include the "hands" whom they employed. The factories are associated, and rightly, with long hours of unremitting labour of men, women and children, with a harsh internal discipline, and a tyrannical repudiation of the workers' right to combine in their own defence. They are accused often enough, too, of being a means of lowering wages and standards of life. But the accusations are overdone. The factory did not create new economic relationships, though it did impose a new discipline. Inevitably, it took over what was already in being. It inherited child labour and women's labour from an immemorial past, just as it inherited the habit of long hours and of hostility to workers' combinations. These things fit quite naturally into a society which employed the press-gang for recruiting purposes and Oliver the spy to gain inside knowledge of the hopes and ambitions of working people. But the factory as such cannot be accused of lowering wages: a comparison with the record of agriculture or mines or frame-work knitting or hand-loom weaving shows conditions worse than those in the factory industries. Besides, the "sweated" industries of which such gloomy revelations were made in the early years of the twentieth century were those which escaped the transforming hand of industrial revolution. It is as well to remember, too, that some of the industrial evils arose from conditions over which the factory owner had no control. The evil of truck was not peculiar to the textile factories; it was common, even usual, in the Sheffield trades, in mining, canal and railway construction. But it is difficult to see how the system could be avoided where work was undertaken in remote places and in days when employers found it difficult to get together the small coin necessary for wage payments.[1] The "tommy shop" described vividly and truly in Disraeli's *Sybil*, was a centre of abuses, but the conditions of the day necessitated the institution of truck though not, of course, the abuse of it. There were, of course, good employers as well as bad ones. Such were Matthew Boulton and Robert Owen. Further, the accusations against the factories were to a large extent made in the heat of controversy, of the great controversy over the Corn Laws:

[1] See G. Unwin, *Samuel Oldnow and the Arkwrights* (1924), p. 179.

they represent the landed proprietor's reply to those who were attacking his privileged position. Even before the great commissions of enquiry, non-partisan evidence is scarcely available.[1] Almost all the familiar descriptions of evil conditions relate to cotton mills. Yet there is no bright spot in the horror of the conditions described in the Report on Mines in 1842, an industry which had been unvisited by experience parallel to that of cotton. Still, even when full allowance has been made for these and other mitigating circumstances, and even when there is a full recognition of the difficulties of transition, there remains unmistakable evidence in the workers' loathing of the new system. It is impossible to deny that that loathing was largely justified. The new discipline robbed the worker of the chance of easing the pace of his work when he felt the strain: it exposed him to a system of exorbitant fines for minor delinquencies. The factory created a wide range of employments but compelled the male worker to share that range with his women-folk and children who were invariably underpaid; it systematized child labour, pauper and free, and exploited it with persistent brutality, creating a proletariat of stunted weaklings.[2] Above all, it accentuated the employer's power over his workpeople, and the employee's powerlessness before his master. There was a tradition, however slender the practice, of governmental concern for the workers' welfare. Apprenticeship, and wage-regulation, had gone or were going; nothing now stood between the man and his master. And the new tyranny, for so it seemed, was that of the self-made man.

It may well be urged that the worker was taking a narrow view, that ultimately he stood to gain rather than lose by the new system. It may be admitted that the prolonged wars robbed him of wage-advantages and of the better

[1] See *Economica*, March 1926, article by W. H. Hutt, which puts a case for the early factories.

[2] B. Bowker, *Lancashire under the Hammer* (1928), p. 99, suggests the continuity into our day of this physical deterioration.

relationships which the new system had it in its power to give, and caused social retrogression. His best advisers, too, were unanimous in their view that the machinery against which he blindly fought was really his friend. Further, the extent of factory employment is easily exaggerated: the typical town-worker of the decade 1820–30 was very far indeed from being a person who performed for a self-made employer in steaming air, with the aid of recently-devised mechanism, operations which would have made his grandfather gape.[1] We may agree that "the idea that an economic movement . . . which was characterized on the one hand by a greater power of production, and on the other by an expanding economic unity could, of itself, be a cause of widespread distress and of social retrogression is a hard one to accept."[2] Yet, the new industrialism did strike the worker as an evil thing of which he was the undeserving victim, and it did produce a set of values which seemed to him to be false. He was never in doubt, whatever the statisticians might say, that it distributed purchasing power in an unjust and economically foolish way. His eyes, his nose and his C3 health told him, too, that the factory town was a poor place to exchange for the country. His traditional indictment of industrial capitalism is not without substance.

By the middle of the nineteenth century half the population lived in urban areas. The railways had accelerated the townwards movement of the steam-power factories, and the proportion of immigrants from the countryside was greater than the proportion of town-born natives. A retrospective glance at any of the new mushroom towns will suffice to show what sort of environment early industrial capitalism was providing for those who in large measure still had fresh memories of country air. A description of Manchester[3]

[1] J. H. Clapham, *An Economic History of Modern Britain* (1927), p. 74.
[2] G. W. Daniels, *The Early English Cotton Industry* (1920), p. 145.
[3] J. P. Kay, *The Moral and Physical Condition of the Working Classes*

points out that "those districts where the poor dwell are of
very recent origin", outlines the dietary of the cotton
workers and shows it as inadequate to the labours undertaken by them in the contaminated atmosphere of their
work-places. It proceeds: "In some districts of the town
exist evils so remarkable as to require more minute description. A portion of low, swampy ground, liable to be frequently inundated, and to constant exhalation, is included
between a high bank over which the Oxford Road passes,
and a bend of the river Medlock, where its course is impeded by weirs. This unhealthy spot lies so low that the
chimneys of its houses, some of them three stories high, are
little above the level of the road. About two hundred of
these habitations are crowded together in an extremely
narrow space, and are inhabited by the lowest Irish. Most
of these houses have also cellars, whose floor is scarcely
elevated above the level of the water flowing in the Medlock.
The soughs are destroyed or out of repair; and these narrow
abodes are in consequence always damp, and on the slightest
rise in the river, which is a frequent occurrence, are flooded
to the depth of several inches. This district has been frequently the haunt of hordes of thieves and desperadoes
who defied the law, and is always inhabited by a class re-
sembling savages in their appetites and habits. It is sur-
rounded on every side by some of the largest factories of the
town, whose chimneys vomit forth dense clouds of smoke,
which hangs heavily over this insalubrious region." Members of the Manchester Board of Health investigating this
region—which a few years later was the birthplace of an
English prime minister—showed the sewers inadequate to
drain off surface water, let alone the slops of two hundred
houses. The privies were found "inaccessible from filth and
numbering only two to 250 people. The cellars, nine to
ten feet square, were inhabited some by ten, some by more,
people each. Back rooms had no ventilation save from front

employed in the Cotton Manufacture in Manchester (1832). The author
was a doctor.

6

rooms. Elsewhere were cess-pools with open grids close to house-doors; narrow streets on a slope down which filthy streams percolate"; and so on *ad nauseam*. Leaving vice, drunkenness and crime on one side, we are given the conclusion "that diseases assume a lower and more chronic type in Manchester than in smaller towns and agricultural districts". The same story has to be related of the other new towns of the industrial revolution. The noisome pages of Chadwick's Report on the Sanitary Condition of the Labouring Population (1842) give substantiating evidence. So much has survived, too, that though we have not yet scheduled a block of back-to-back houses as a historical monument to be safeguarded by the Board of Works, there would be no difficulty in finding abundance of suitable specimens.

It is easy to point out the speed with which the towns had grown, even to remember the meanness of mediaeval towns. The worst thing, perhaps, that can be said of these conditions is that they were permissible. So far had local government decayed, so little adequate was the reform of the municipal corporations in 1835, and so bitterly disliked was the Public Health campaign of the forties, that they prevailed long after their unworthiness had been demonstrated. It is probably true that in the towns it was the speculative builder rather than the employer who rushed up houses in unpaved and undrained streets and courts: he had to crowd them together to make a profit at all, as rents were advancing rapidly. The time had not yet come for the establishment of a social code protective of that rather helpless body, the community.

But retrogression might have been avoided. Street Improvement Acts had been common between 1785 and 1800: Manchester widened streets that were described in 1775 as "no better than a common dunghill" and made some improvements in water supply, lighting and policing; Liverpool widened streets and spent much on public buildings, though it was less active in improving its water supply or eliminating cellar-dwellings. It seems likely that the industrial towns were willing to give their central areas a dignified façade, but not to deal with the poorer quarters. There "the constant influx of people had to be housed and housed as cheaply as possible"[1]—always the most expensive way of satisfying a primary need. Herein, if it be true, lies a chief count in the reckoning against the new industrialism. A process of economic expansion which was cheapening commodities, increasing employment and making fortunes should not have been conditional on working-class degradation. That it was so is an established fact, whether the explanation be the rapacity of jerry-builders and ground-landlords, the inheritance of low standards of town life and a weak set of local governmental institutions, or a devastating influx of pauperized Irish.

[1] M. C. Buer, *Health, Wealth and Population, 1760–1815* (1926), p. 231.

CHAPTER VIII

THE RESPONSE OF LABOUR

THE response of the workers to the great industrial changes covered all the possible varieties of protest from undisguised violence to constructive organization. When the character of the industrial revolution is being assessed, this response is evidence of the first importance. The life of the workers was affected far more drastically than the life of any other class. There is no vast difference between either affluence or destitution in one age and another; nor does the lot of those to whom a comfortable security is assured fluctuate greatly. But the humbler folk in any community live so near the verge of calamity that even small changes in their standard of livelihood or in their immediate environment have big effects. It is scarcely surprising, therefore, to discover intermittent hostility to machinery, which, if it made employment in the long run, saved it in the short, a permanent dislike of the swollen power of employers, and, combined therewith, a strongly-held labour theory of value, however rudimentary its expression. The generations of workmen who lived through the reign of George III and the Free Trade struggle had witnessed the enclosures and the gradual annihilation of village industries: in many counties they had learned to rely on the Poor Law for wage-assistance; they had, like other classes, filled up the armies in the wars and returned to an impoverished world when peace came: they were distrusted or misunderstood by undemocratic governments, ready to employ industrial spies to their undoing and to dragoon them by a lavish use of the forces of the Crown. If leading statesmen failed to appreciate the true character of the developments afoot, workingpeople, denied educational facilities, could scarcely be expected to have a wider vision.

The record of violence is a long one. Sometimes it achieved more than a local significance, as in the Luddite risings of 1811 and 1812, or the wholly unnecessary Battle of Peterloo on the site of later Cobdenite triumphs in Manchester in 1819; or the Labourers' Revolts in the rural counties in 1830. More commonly the disturbances indicated the temper of a particular district, as when Arkwright's machinery was destroyed in 1779, or Cartwright's in 1791. It may well be that in Yorkshire one result of this unconcealed hostility was the delay in adopting machinery in the woollen manufacture.[1] In Lancashire, too, machine-breaking caused the migration of several industrial units outside the county.

But violence left no permanent influence on the English labour movement, however large it loomed in the eyes of contemporaries. Nor was it typical of it.

Far more significant than machine-breaking was the rise of labour organizations. The trade union is scarcely the child of the industrial revolution: it is to be found in thirteenth-century London, in the seventeenth-century journeymen's associations, in the earlier as well as the later eighteenth century, though often disguised as a friendly society. When the industrial capitalist appeared, the trade union appeared also. If it was driven underground by the numerous anti-combination Acts which led up to the better-known prohibition of 1799–1800, it was certainly not extinguished thereby, perhaps not even seriously handicapped. The growth of a trade union movement went on in despite of them. It may be recalled that Francis Place, who engineered the repeal of this legislation in 1824, declared that it encouraged rather than prevented the formation of workers' combinations. In any case its effective use by employers was not automatic and it was no more severe in its penalties than earlier Acts.[2] A more powerful foe than

---

[1] Halévy, *History of the English People in 1815* (English translation, 1924), p. 262.

[2] See D. George, "The Combination Laws Reconsidered", in

either legislation or action at common law, it would seem, was the progress of machinery. An example of this is the experience of the woolcombers, who maintained a successful trade-club in the earlier eighteenth century and onwards, until in the mid-nineteenth century the coming of a combing machine reduced it to insignificance.[1] The unions, or the benefit societies as which they sometimes masqueraded, were indeed in a difficult position. They were regarded as conspiracies before the law; they were prohibited by Act of Parliament; they could only rarely become more than local trade clubs; the statutes upon which labour might have relied such as the Elizabethan enforcement of apprenticeship were rapidly becoming obsolete; the process of industrial change was handing over particular industrial functions to machines, or to women and children—the very face of industry, that is, was changing; the proceedings of trade unions were quickening the demand for mechanical inventions and yet if they did not combine and act to protect themselves, they would become the victims of the employers' rapacity or of the competition of cheaper labour from the countryside or from Ireland. It is not surprising, then, that both before and after the Repeal of the Combination Acts, by which they became legally permissible bodies, unions came into being and were snuffed out by a strike, whether successful or not, or by a bad burst of unemployment, or by attack through the law courts.

Yet the needs of labour were envisaged with some clarity, and heroic efforts were made to build up powerful organizations. It has been estimated that in the early forties there were less than 100,000 trade unionists in the country, but figures cannot adequately represent either the effort made or its significance. In the early thirties, inspired by the doctrines of Robert Owen, attempts were made to build up

Economic Journal, Economic History Supplement, May 1927. The findings of this article are scarcely consistent with the Reports on Artisans and Machinery of 1824.

[1] J. H. Clapham, *An Economic History of Modern Britain* (1927), p. 206.

national organizations expressive of working-class solidarity
and of a more constructive attitude towards industrialism.
In 1829 John Doherty led the way to the foundation of a
Grand General Union of All the Operative Spinners of the
United Kingdom, in 1830 to a National Association for the
Protection of Labour. There were big schemes, too, among
builders, potters, woollen workers, miners, and a Metropolitan Trades Union was organized among the various
London societies. All this activity culminated in the initiation in 1833 of the Grand National Consolidated Trades
Union, the title given in 1834 to the project Owen had
formed of a Grand National Moral Union of the Productive Classes of Great Britain and Ireland. The purpose
of this body was to end the era of capitalism by establishing
a system of universal co-operation under workers' control.
Before even its formal title had been adopted, the Grand
National was engaged in supporting the workers of Derby
against an employers' attack; in other towns a similar
situation quickly arose. The government followed the
employers' example. They gave an explicit and discreditable
approval of a savage sentence of seven years' transportation passed on farm labourers in Tolpuddle for administer-
ing oaths in the enrolment ceremony for new members.
But internal weaknesses as much as external attacks and
sectional strikes brought the end of the Grand National.
It had had a few months of crowded life, but had been able
to confront the walls of the capitalist Jericho with little
more than trumpetings. Owen set to work with other
instruments to establish the "new moral world", and the
unions which survived the disastrous and premature
schemes of 1830–34 turned to less millennial plans. They had
to learn in disillusion the necessity of the humdrum work of
intensive organization—to build up a series of strong units
which time and leadership would fuse and inspire with a
sense of purpose and a knowledge of possible directions.

The failure of this idealistic trades-unionism was not
surprising. It was the old story of attempting to run before

the walking process had been learned. The masterful industrialists, too, were flushed with the victory of parliamentary reform, won in 1832, and they had gained the initiative in the field of industrial warfare. Though they were not yet more successful than their employees in achieving unity, circumstances were all in their favour. Yet this phase of Owenite influence was not insignificant. It did the negative service of pointing out weaknesses: it showed the essential conditions of success; it led directly into Chartism, which, ostensibly a failure, was in a very real sense the "growing pains" stage of the labour movement. The three-fold character of the labour movement, industrial, political and co-operative, was visualized as the result of the experience of the thirties and forties, for it was found then, if painfully, that the transformation of the new order could only be achieved by a three-fold advance. It is true, of course, that Socialism—an uneasy bed-fellow of consumers' co-operation—had already won many adherents. But so had other gospels. In the Chartist era, "working men had forced upon their attention the pros and cons of trade unionism, industrial unionism, socialism, co-operative ownership of land, land nationalization, co-operative distribution, co-operative production, co-operative ownership of credit, franchise reform, electoral reform, woman suffrage, factory legislation, poor law reform, municipal reform, free trade, freedom of the press, freedom of thought, the nationalist idea, industrial assurance, building societies, and many other ideas."[1] In all this eager canvassing of ideas, trade unionism was shown to be not a short cut to a new Jerusalem, or even to a more limited earthly paradise; it was realized that its functions were protection, and advance where possible, in the narrower sphere of wages and conditions of employment.

The co-operative movement went through a cycle of experiences similar to that of trade-unionism. Self-help societies or stores came into being, commonly with the

[1] J. West, *A History of the Chartist Movement* (1920), p. 6.

philanthropic aid of middle-class sympathizers, in different parts of the country: they were at best protests against high prices or unemployment. It was not till Robert Owen's idealism permeated important sections of the working-classes that a co-operative movement of more than local significance took shape. This movement had big aims. It envisaged the establishment of "villages of co-operation", of communities of people, where, as No. 147 of the Social Hymns for the use of the Friends of the Rational System of Society put it:

> "Nor *mine* nor *thine* in social life is known,
> But universal *ours* there sways alone:
> Our end our aim—that end the good of all,
> With us no rich, no poor; no rise, no fall."

The evils of the age were to have no place in these self-governing communities. The opening of stores was the workers' first step to Owenite harmonies; thus a capital fund could be built up for a future community and a capitalistic evil eliminated at one and the same time. In the same spirit skilled workers managed to establish small co-operative workshops, "Union shops", whose output could be sold at the store, or at an Exchange Bazaar, as by London co-operators in 1830, or at the larger National Equitable Labour Exchange established in 1832, or similar agencies in some of the larger provincial towns.

Owen's leadership was, in fact, drawing working-class energies in a number of directions simultaneously. For besides propagandist societies, educational and co-operative, union shops, labour exchanges, co-operative stores, and trade unions, there was launched an organized demand for an eight-hours day in 1833, this being the prime purpose of the National Regeneration Society. All these activities were to be fused in the final attack on capitalism envisaged as the great purpose of the Grand National Consolidated Trades Union. Just as more modest trade unionism issued from the debacle of that great project, so did a more utilitarian co-operation. The co-operative idea was with

difficulty kept alive in the succeeding decade: it was signi-
ficantly revived when the Toad Lane store was opened in
Rochdale in 1844. But it was revived with a difference. The
Rochdale plan was immediately practical and ultimately
idealistic. It provided immediately for the sale of necessaries to its supporters and for the division of profits in
proportion to purchases; it aimed ultimately at the establishment of communities on the Owenite plan. If the bird-
in-the-hand of the "divi." has counted for more than the
bird-in-the-bush of the ideal community, that does not say
that the Co-operative movement has lost faith in the ideal
of a co-operative commonwealth. On the basis of the
Rochdale plan it has ever since 1844 been building up a substantial structure, and it has been reserved for our own day
to see it accept the logic of its past and take its place in a
mature and ambitious labour movement with a united front.

The Chartist movement is another of the manifestations
of the labour reaction to industrialism. Showing the same
splendid courage and the same power of rapid improvisa-
tion, the Chartists represent the more political aspirations
of the working classes. It is difficult to write briefly either
about Chartist aims or Chartist activities, so various were
they. No doubt most Chartists looked to political reform as
a means to the end of economic improvement. Chartism in
that sense was a "bread and butter" movement; but it was
more also. It gathered momentum from all the consciously
felt grievances and from that less adequately expressed but
none the less real dissatisfaction with "the system" which is
the mark of all revolutionary movements. As various as
their enthusiasms were the Chartists themselves—middle-
class, artisan and unskilled; urban and rural; agricultural
and industrial and professional. In practice the Chartists
never achieved concentration of purpose or action; neither
in 1839, when the Convention was in session and a "Sacred
Month" of abstention from labour was planned as the
reply to Parliament's rejection of the first Petition; nor in
1842 when the complete Suffrage Movement momentarily

united the various groups in the presentation of a second Petition; nor in the rally of 1848 when insurrection was commonly expected to follow the rejection of the third Petition. There was never substantial likelihood of results proportionate to hopes. Yet a steady demand for education and, above all, experience came to working-class leaders as the result of Chartism. They were thrown back by the Chartist defeats upon trade unionism and co-operation, and brought into touch with Continental socialists, especially Marx and Engels.

Movements may not always be measured by their immediate success. These labour movements won few victories, but they gained a sense of purpose and in the end a plan. It is easy to regard Owenite optimism in a superior way, yet from the inspiration of the Owenite vision the labour movement acquired ideals, a sense of unity and a regard for the immediately possible. The modern Labour movement has no need to be ashamed or forgetful of its parentage.

CHAPTER IX

GOVERNMENT POLICY

DURING the industrial revolution Parliament was not representative of the mass of the nation. Governmental powers were exercised by an aristocracy which, because it was an aristocracy, had necessarily a sectional outlook. George III tried to revive the limited powers left to the monarch by the Glorious Revolution, but he had neither the capacity nor the vision of the benevolent despots who succeeded elsewhere in modernizing their states. His incursion into politics was a parenthesis. The landed aristocracy was supreme. Lords and Commons were alike its stronghold, the House of Lords being no sleeping partner in the business of government. Seats in the House of Commons could always be purchased. Parties were not yet defined in the way which is familiar to us; they were rather cliques or factions than parties. What we call corruption prevailed from top to bottom of the political system. Efficient organs of administration were not yet developed. The London outlook dominated the political life of the country quite disproportionately. Local government was the affair of magistrates or of little, often self-elected, corporations, or of special statutory bodies. Clearly, a sympathetic understanding of the great economic changes and of their social effects could scarcely be expected. When Cobbett told the labourer that he could hope for nothing from an unreformed Parliament, he was telling him the truth. Had Parliament been a democratic body, it would have known how to interpret the rick-burning, the vitriol-throwing and the machine-breaking which it knew only how to punish. Fundamental reform could not issue from an unreformed Parliament. This does not say that the aristocracy did not render good services; they did—especially when their interests and those of the nation coincided. But government tended to be paternal or sentimental or merely repressive. The Speenhamland methods of poor relief, Game Laws, Enclosure procedure, the Six Acts, the Combination Acts, are positive expressions of the mind of the class which wielded the powers of government; negative expressions of it are the inability to appreciate the need of popular education, to measure the extent and causes of popular distress and discontent, and to discover the urgency of enforcing some minimum standards of public health practice.

Three great branches of public policy are selected for examination, namely, poverty, employment in factories, and the freeing of trade.

THE POOR LAW

It is not to be supposed that the problem of poverty was a new one, or that the administration of the Poor Law had ever been uniform. The outlines of the Elizabethan system, on which later practice was based, had been clear. That system was one of relief for those who could not help themselves, and of employment for those who could work but were not in fact doing so. In accordance with it there had been established in most counties Houses of Correction or "Bridewells" for miscreant paupers, and in towns and rural areas Workhouses or Houses of Industry, for the unemployed poor. The workhouses for long retained their original purpose of "setting the poor on work", but they were sometimes used also as a shelter for the aged and helpless. In addition many parishes had adopted out-relief as a means of assisting both the impotent and the able-bodied. An Act of 1782, Gilbert's Act, encouraged this development, and under the pressure of growing rural distress, the system of out-relief was given an enormous extension. The Berkshire magistrates, meeting at Speenhamland in 1795, drew up a bread scale, whereby wages were supplemented from the rates. This Berkshire method was widely adopted in what were regarded as circumstances of emergency, but it lasted down to 1834. The workhouses and poor-houses deteriorated, while out-relief was made to include what should have been a considerable part of the country's wage-bill. Poor rates mounted and the administration became chaotic. A few examples will show how things were.

In one parish the same person acted as overseer, assistant overseer, warden, rate-collector, and workhouse master, was in business as butcher, farmer, quarrier and carman, determined the rates and functioned as constable. Asked if he gave the children a good education, he replied, "God forbid! all the six and thirty years I have been overseer, I never gave children no larning." Not one of the poor children in Mr. Parker's parish could read or write.

In another parish the overseer held office for eleven years; a large landowner and farmer, he kept the parish books in his own shop, to the accounts of which they were closely related. Paupers were always informed at the vestry that its decisions would be communicated to them at the shop; and they were dealt with at the vestry according to their docility at the shop. Some £1,200 a year from the rates passed thus over the overseer's own counter: people complained that his prices were forty per cent above the usual prices; what the vestry did not grant, he himself awarded as "casual relief", of which also the record lay on the counter. The method of making a rate was simple: he put on the church door the notice, "A rate wanted", and it was granted. The vicar and rival shopkeepers kept silent because they were left out of the rate altogether. When dismissed, after 1834, he committed suicide. Convictions in this parish were treble those of neighbouring villages.

Parish books often showed interesting entries. "To John Bell, for cutting his throaght, 12s." "To William Dormer, ill (through drink), 5s." "To Elizabeth W., a present for her kindness to her father, 5s." "Paid for men and boys stand-

ing in the pound, 6 days, £6 7s. 0d." The enforcement of
labour on the roads or at other tasks was commonly
farcical: "I passed twenty-seven of them all fast asleep . . ."
or, "they were playing at marbles till the weather was fine
enough to admit of their going to work . . ." or, "the *work*
on the roads was lying under the hedge. . . ."

The paupers, infirm and able-bodied alike, were commonly better off than those in regular employment. The
Speenhamland system, therefore, demoralized labourers
and farmers, and was a burden to all who could not in
some way profit by it. As a method of avoiding the payment
of reasonable wages, nothing much better could have been
devised. But at its worst it was an expenditure easily within
the means of the nation, and it is certain that some method
of easing the high-price situation was necessary .

A change came quickly after the advent of a reformed
House of Commons. In 1832 a Royal Commission examined
the system and in 1834 the Poor Law Amendment Act was
passed. The parish as the administrative unit gave way to
the union of parishes; actual administration was supervised,
and as far as possible standardized, by a new central Poor
Law Board of three Commissioners; union workhouses
were to be provided at which the able unemployed would
labour for a living always meaner than that of the lowest
independent workers. Business methods and economy were
to replace corruption, inefficiency and wastefulness; supervision and audited accounts were to do as much as the
elected Boards of Guardians to assure the excision of the
malignant growth of idle and often pleasurable pauperism.
This much-belauded measure pleased the ratepayer and
angered the poor. Presumably it was necessary. Yet the
pauper had not been to blame for his poverty and it was
unwise to reduce the mobility of labour by narrowing the
conditions under which a settlement could be acquired.
From the point of view of the worker, poverty which springs
from unemployment is not fitly dealt with by the Poor Law
at all. All experience subsequent to 1834 goes to show that

he is right. In 1909, when a new Royal Commission on the Poor Laws reported, powerful voices expressed their agreement with him.

FACTORY LEGISLATION

The rise of factories was a godsend to overseers embarrassed with a swollen supply of pauper children. But the factories quickly achieved a bad name. Hence a "Health and Morals of Apprentices Act" was passed in 1802, by which pauper apprentices in cotton mills were promised a twelve-hour working day, the discontinuance of night work, a yearly suit of clothes, a monthly attendance at church, a biennial whitewashing of the factory walls, separate sleeping apartments, with not more than two in a bed, for boys and girls, and instruction in reading, writing and arithmetic. This was the first of the Factory Acts, but it mattered little as pauper apprenticeship was rapidly declining.

Appropriately the Act of 1802 had originated with Sir Robert Peel (father of the Prime Minister), the reputed author of the mass-apprenticeship of pauper children. The next step was due to Robert Owen. Owen had proved that good conditions were consistent with profits: he had won a reputation as the Henry Ford of his day and was listened to respectfully. But the Act of 1819 fell short of his proposals and his practice. It prohibited the employment in cotton mills of children under nine and limited the working hours for all under sixteen to a daily twelve. Neither this Act nor its two subsequent amending Acts got to the heart of the factory problem or provided adequate administrative machinery. The Act of 1833 made provision for the appointment of Factory Inspectors, but it did nothing for the regulation of adult labour, and only added the limitation of the hours of workers under eighteen to sixty-nine a week. A vigorous Ten Hours movement was initiated, and enlisted the support of Sadler and then Lord Ashley, afterwards Earl of Shaftesbury. Stimulated by the impression produced by the revelations of conditions in the mines, and guided by the reports of the Factory Inspectors, Parliament passed the Act of 1844. This important measure established the half-time system for children, gave women as well as young persons the twelve-hour day, and enforced the fencing of machinery. John Bright's argument against this Act was that still worse conditions prevailed in other industries, which was quite believable. But the opposition failed to win their case, even though they had the support of economists like Senior, and had to endure in 1847 the victory of the Ten Hours agitation. The extension of factory legislation to non-textile industries and the scheduling of dangerous trades belong to the second half of the century. Yet what had been done in the textile factories and in the abolition in 1842 of the underground employment of women and children was important. It provided relief here, and a precedent which other countries have since followed.

FREE TRADE

Broadly interpreted, the Free Trade movement was concerned to substitute for authoritative regulation in all spheres of economic life a régime of individualism. Accordingly dying or dead statutes were repealed and an attack was made on surviving restrictions even though vested interests and long-established modes of thought strongly supported them. In this way apprenticeship as a compulsory system was removed (1813), usury laws were repealed (1833 and 1854), the ban on trade unions was abandoned (1824–1825). But it was more difficult to deal with the complicated network of import and export duties. Here the fiscal needs of the state had to be considered and the protected industries to be treated carefully. Free Trade had to come gradually, therefore, and by various routes. The export of machinery was freed (1825 and 1844); the East India Company lost its monopoly of trade with India (1813) and with the East (1833); the Navigation Acts were relaxed (1823) and then repealed (1849). Under Huskisson a great reform of the cumbersome tariff was effected between 1822 and 1824. Duties on raw materials were got rid of under Peel in 1842 and 1845, and duties on partly and fully manufactured goods were in the same years either reduced or abolished, save for a few of which Gladstone purged the Customs list in 1853 and 1860. There remained, then, a carefully selected and compact group of articles of common consumption on which duties were levied for revenue purposes.

Many of these steps towards Free Trade were regarded as non-controversial. New tendencies of thought had almost obliterated older views of the functions of the state. The commercial, financial and industrial leaders of the country were convinced of the necessity of the removal of all restrictions which might impede their progress. But there was one question on which opinion was not clear—that of the validity of protection to agriculture. The old rulers of the country joined issue with the new in a battle over the Corn Laws and the result of that battle was largely to determine the balance of political power in the House of Commons. In 1846 the abolition of the Corn Laws was decided upon and agriculture was left to its fate as an unsheltered industry.

The question of the Corn Laws filled a very large place in public discussion after 1815. For earlier generations the Corn Laws had had different aims from the protection of the agricultural interest merely. Their original scope was three-fold: to obtain for consumers good supplies at fair prices; to serve the interests of producers, whether landlords or farmers; to amplify the strength of the state through enlarged revenues, greater supplies and a busy merchant marine. The Corn Laws mattered little enough before or when the cotton lords attacked them: the anti-corn-law apostles were fervent rather than convincing in their analysis of the evils of protection to agriculture. The truth was that abundant supplies were not available from outside sources and that their costs of transport necessitated high prices. The economist makes it clear that even a slight shortage of supplies of such a commodity as corn, in universal and incessant demand as a first need, brings, quite inevitably, the disturbing accompaniment of high prices. The floods of popular oratory deflected public discussion into rather unreal channels. The social reactions of economic change *were* being discussed by the anti-capitalist economists —poor relations of Ricardo but close kinsmen of Marx— and the labour movement, in its Chartist and other forms. That discussion, however turgid and elementary it may seem to later generations, was of first-rate significance in its day. It might have led to the formulation of standards of social welfare or plans of purposive reform. As it was, the masterful propagandists of Manchester got the ear of all classes. Discussion then turned round the important but lesser issues of the cost of living and of manufacturing. Battle was joined between the aristocracies of land and cotton for pre-eminence in Parliament, from which factory "hand" and landless labourer alike were excluded. Later history goes to show that this absorbing struggle was largely irrelevant to the condition of the England that devoted itself to it. Westminster had to wait for new voices before it could handle social issues imaginatively. Franchise reforms admitted the town worker to political responsibilities in 1867, the village labourer in 1884, women and "children in arms" in 1918, and "flappers" in this present year (1928). The Corn Laws were abandoned in 1846, yet the farmers had a long innings of unexpected prosperity. And in the seventies an era of reforms—education, housing, public health, old age pensions, unemployment, workmen's compensation, and the rest, belated but significant—set in on socialistic lines. The correctives to economic individualism and in-dustrial capitalism—trade unionism, municipal trading, consumers' co-operation—were gaining strength while Cobdenism, a wider gospel than mere free trade, was losing it in the years following 1846. It would be unfair to suggest that England paid too heavy a price for the anti-corn-law agitation. It was perhaps worth while to let England's thought follow Manchester's lead for a season, provided it did not become an ineradicable habit. But it is a pity that more notice was not taken of Adam Smith's revealing and to this age quaint judgment of corn laws in general. "The laws concerning corn," he wrote, "may everywhere be compared to the laws concerning religion. The people feel themselves so much interested in what relates either to their subsistence in this life, or to their happiness in a life to come, that government must yield to their prejudices, and, in order to preserve the public tranquillity, establish that system which they approve of. It is on this account, perhaps, that we so seldom find a reasonable system established with regard to either of these two capital objects."

CHAPTER X

EPILOGUE

"WE have no thread," wrote a great historian, "through the enormous intricacy of modern politics except the idea of progress towards more perfect and assured freedom and the divine right of free men." Such a statement might equally be made of the social and economic changes of the eighteenth and nineteenth centuries.

By 1850 a well-defined phase of economic development was complete. Steam-power and machinery had won their victories, even though small production and the sweater's workshop still tenaciously maintained themselves on the outskirts of the factory. The technique of big-scale manufacture was in large measure understood, and appropriate specialists in its various functions were being rapidly defined. Violence had passed from the workers' mind as a possible argument against employers. The farm labourer had tightened his belt, and become stoical about the workhouse as the probable home of his declining years; the agony of the hand-loom weavers was passing with their final extinction; the Irish migrant was "off to Philadelphia" instead of Lancashire; the drab northern and Midland towns had settled down to a placid toleration of their meagre amenities. "It would be a rather difficult matter," said Hugh Miller in 1847, "to make a novel out of an English tour. The country, measured by days' journeys, has grown nine-tenths smaller than it was in the times of Fielding and Smollett. The law has become too strong for Captain Macheath the highwayman. . . . The journeyer by moonlight who accidentally loses his road . . . merely encounters some suspicious gamekeeper, taking his night-rounds in behalf of the Squire's pheasants. . . . Society in England, in the present day, exists, like the thawing iceberg, in a transition state, and presents its consequent shiftings of aspect and changes of feature."

The age of personal adventure had not gone by; it had suffered a change of form. The romantic figures now were the self-help heroes of Samuel Smiles, and the George Hudsons and Leopold Redpaths of the railway world. The financial editor of *The Times* wrote a volume called *Facts, Failures and Frauds*, which he described as "in some degree supplemental" to his histories of the commercial crises of 1847–48 and 1857–58. But the character of a civilization cannot be gathered from its romantic or exceptional figures. It is revealed in the lives of the typical and the hum-drum— the northern manufacturer, competent, self-assured and complacent, who was content with an order of things which allowed him to buy in the cheapest and sell in the dearest market; the urban artisan, for whom religion was no more than an undefined hereditary prejudice, work a monotonous round of disciplined toil, and leisure at best the Sunday trip to a country alehouse; the tenant-farmer, enfranchised in 1832 but as a tenant-at-will, the political vassal of his land- lord; the labourer of the farm and the mine, politically voiceless and socially isolated. It was a civilization that had strength without grace.

But if early Victorian civilization lacked colour, it did not lack vitality. People worked hard and saved hard. They passed on the technique and the products of the new in- dustrialism to other countries; they exported their capital, and a considerable fraction of their population, so that a big contribution to the establishment of a world economy was made. They effected small improvements in their own internal organization, educational, political and social, so that a democratic varnish was given to the solid middle- class structure. Above all, they rapidly pushed on with the task of enlarging industry and trade on the lines laid down. The Great Exhibition of 1851 showed a solidity of achieve- ment which could not be mistaken.

But there were uneasy voices. John Stuart Mill declared, a shade rhetorically, that "it is questionable if all the mechanical inventions yet made have lightened the day's toil of any human being." He cast doubt on the final superiority of the progressive society by stating a case for the stationary society. Obscurer critics continued to demand a socialistic millennium, though there was as yet no need to take notice of them. At any rate, it was clear that the individualist philosophy did not command universal assent, and that the minority not included in the greatest number, whose greatest happiness was the recognized aim of the state, would some day become restive. Victorian civilization was making the rich richer more quickly than it was helping the poor. Undercurrents of thought and dissatisfaction were gradually leading to collectivist legislation. When the tide set in that direction in the 1870s, arrears of social reform legislation were rapidly made up. That legislation marked the end of the *laissez faire* era and the dawning of new conceptions of social justice.

The typical institutions of the Victorian era were the limited liability company and the voluntary association. By the agency of the former, the difficulties of capital recruitment were removed. Industrial and commercial undertakings could expand in accordance with opportunity: the complete mobility of financial resources enabled new countries, tropical and temperate, to be "opened up". It was a short move from the limited liability company to the combine and the investment trust, and to that industrial concentration which made the worker, like the soldier, a mere number in the industrial army. If the worker so placed lacked the soldier's security of tenure, he gained anonymity and impersonal relationships with his employer, and so the chance of making a business contract instead of a mere bargain about his conditions of employment. From the limited company, too, there issued the "absentee" shareholder whose undertaking is managed by specialists and who submits to the process of "involuntary saving", by which the business institution reduces its reliance upon individual "abstinence" or "waiting" for its funds of fresh capital. Private enterprise thus loses its earlier features. Joint Stock institutions begin to show "a trend, when they have reached a certain size and age, to approximate to the status of public corporations." At this stage, when owners of the capital and managers of the concern are almost entirely dissociated, big enterprise tends "to socialize itself."[1]

The other typical institution was the voluntary association. Such bodies have been readily formed in the age of industrialism for a multitude of purposes. They have created and led opinion. By their force they have overcome the inertia of parliaments and enabled the insignificant common man, provided he has a sense of purpose and some energy, to make his contribution to the causes he has deemed important. The greater leisure, which was ultimately to issue from the industrial revolution, and the freedom to think and to organize are, in the last analysis, its leading gifts. They enable us to deal with the present in a constructive way.

Concealed in the efforts of our Cromptons and Watts was a world economy. The rise of Lancashire did not damage Yorkshire; nor did the rise of Germany or the United States ultimately harm England. But the spread of international economic co-operation is as yet only faintly outlined.

[1] J. M. Keynes, *End of Laissez Faire* (1926), p. 42.

For Product Safety Concerns and Information please contact our EU
representative GPSR@taylorandfrancis.com
Taylor & Francis Verlag GmbH, Kaufingerstraße 24, 80331 München, Germany

www.ingramcontent.com/pod-product-compliance
Lightning Source LLC
Chambersburg PA
CBHW060446240326
41599CB00062B/5275

* 9 7 8 1 0 3 2 9 0 6 2 5 6 *